Helping Your Family Thrive

A Practical Guide to Parenting With Positive Behavior Support

by

Meme Hieneman, Ph.D., BCBA
Home and Community Positive Behavior Support Network
Palm Harbor, Florida

Sarah Fefer, Ph.D., BCBA
The University of Massachusetts Amherst

Shane Isley, M.S., BCBA
West Coast Behavioural Consultants, Ltd. (WCB)
Vancouver, British Columbia

and

Missy Sieders, B.A.
PEAK Parent Training and Information Center
Colorado Springs, Colorado

Baltimore • London • Sydney

Paul H. Brookes Publishing Co.
Post Office Box 10624
Baltimore, Maryland 21285-0624
USA

www.brookespublishing.com

Typeset by Progressive Publishing Services, Inc.
Manufactured in the United States of America by
Integrated Books International, Inc., Dulles, Virginia.

All examples in this book are composites. Any similarity to actual individuals or circumstances is coincidental, and no implications should be inferred.

Library of Congress Cataloging-in-Publication Data

Names: Hieneman, Meme, author. | Fefer, Sarah, author. | Isley, Shane,
  author. | Sieders, Missy, author.
Title: Helping your family thrive : a practical guide to parenting with
  positive behavior support / by Meme Hieneman, Ph.D., Sarah Fefer, Ph.D., BCBA,
  Shane Isley, M.S., BCBA, Missy Sieders, B.A.
Description: Baltimore, Maryland : Paul H. Brookes Publishing Co., [2022] |
  Includes bibliographical references and index.
Identifiers: LCCN 2021059942 (print) | LCCN 2021059943 (ebook) |
  ISBN 9781681255675 (paperback) | ISBN 9781681255682 (epub) |
  ISBN 9781681255699 (pdf)
Subjects: LCSH: Parenting. | Behavior modification. | Families.
Classification: LCC HQ755.8 .H5197 2022 (print) | LCC HQ755.8 (ebook) |
  DDC 649/.64—dc23/eng/20220111
LC record available at https://lccn.loc.gov/2021059942
LC ebook record available at https://lccn.loc.gov/2021059943

British Library Cataloguing in Publication data are available from the British Library.

2026   2025   2024   2023   2022

10   9   8   7   6   5   4   3   2   1

Contents

Contents

About the Downloads

Purchasers of this book may download, print, and/or photocopy the worksheets and information-gathering tools in the text for clinical, educational, and personal use.

To access the materials that come with this book:

1. Go to the Brookes Download Hub: http://downloads.brookespublishing.com

2. Register to create an account (or log in with an existing account).

3. Filter or search for the book title *Helping Your Family Thrive: A Practical Guide to Parenting With Positive Behavior Support.*

About the Authors

This book is written by three board certified behavior analysts and a parent/professional who all have extensive experience working with families. We collaborated on this book because we share similar values regarding respecting the uniqueness and integrity of families while using evidence-based practices to improve family decision making. Here is a bit more about each of the authors.

Meme Hieneman, Ph.D., BCBA, Consultant with Positive Behavior Support Applications, Faculty Member at Purdue University Global, and President of the Home and Community Positive Behavior Support Network, Palm Harbor, Florida

Meme was a consultant, researcher, educator, and advocate who worked with organizations that support children with significant behavioral challenges and provide information and resources through teaching and nonprofit work. She was married for more than 30 years and had two young adult sons. Meme had a doctorate in special education and was certified as a behavior analyst. She published a variety of articles, chapters, and three books. She developed a comprehensive video and training package on positive behavior support (PBS) for parents of children with autism and other developmental disabilities and was a regular contributor to *Parenting Special Needs Magazine.*

Meme worked with children with severe behavioral challenges and their families for more than 30 years. She was a residential program manager; behavior specialist for a school district; staff member for a program assisting families and professionals of children with autism; adjunct instructor at the University of South Florida (USF); director of a state-wide PBS project helping schools to implement proactive, evidence-based interventions; co-training coordinator for the National Research and Training Center on PBS; research director of the Positive Family Intervention Project at USF; director and developer of the applied behavior analysis (ABA) and autism programs at All Children's Hospital; and Co-Principal Investigator of a National Institutes of Health-research study focused on behavioral parent education. She last taught masters' level courses in ABA, consulted with agencies that provide family-focused behavioral support, and led a nonprofit organization called the Home and Community Positive Behavior Support Network (https://hcpbs.org/).

Sarah Fefer, Ph.D., BCBA, Associate Professor of School Psychology at the University of Massachusetts Amherst, Department of Student Development, School Psychology program

Sarah is a researcher, trainer, behavior analyst, and systems consultant supporting children, youth, families, and schools in meeting the needs of students with challenging behavior. Sarah has worked in the area of PBS since 2012 when she completed an advanced practicum at All Children's Hospital. Family-focused behavioral intervention was her area of emphasis during her doctoral training in school psychology at the University of South Florida. Sarah was under the supervision of Meme Hieneman, who delivered and evaluated the outcomes of informational workshops and intensive PBS to families experiencing a wide range of challenging child behavior. After her graduate training, Sarah moved to Massachusetts and worked as a doctoral intern in specialized schools for individuals with brain injuries and autism spectrum disorders. She provided training in proactive positive behavioral interventions to teachers, families, and residential staff. Sarah's applied experiences with youth and families across school, hospital, and clinic settings contribute to her current work focused on family-focused strategies as the key to student success.

Sarah is now Associate Professor of School Psychology at the University of Massachusetts Amherst, where she has trained graduate students and engaged in research and service delivery related to PBS for families since 2013. Her most recent projects focus on providing family education through schools, teaching parents to prevent and manage challenging behavior at home. This project involves implementing multiple types of family education using a multitiered model, with some proactive strategies available for all families with children in the school and more intensive education offered to families of students with more significant challenging behaviors.

Shane Isley, M.S., BCBA, Consultant with the Performance Thinking Network and Founder/Director of West Coast Behavioural Consultants, Ltd (WCB)

Shane is an entrepreneur, organizational performance consultant, and behavior analyst who earned his bachelor's and master's degrees in behavior analysis from the University of North Texas. After graduate school, Shane moved back to the Pacific Northwest with his heart set on utilizing behavioral science to make socially significant changes in the places where people spend the most of their time—home and work. In 2007, he founded West Coast Behavioral Consultants, which housed two divisions—Optimal and Blueprints. Optimal focused on performance improvement within organizations. Blueprints focused on intensive family-centered intervention for families with children at risk of out-of-home placement due to their severe challenging behavior. In 2010, Shane founded a sister company (WCB) in Vancouver, British Columbia, Canada.

Applying his expertise in PBS to children and families' needs, Shane and his team of highly skilled practitioners collaborated closely with Dr. Hieneman to build a rigorous family-centered behavioral intervention program, including Family Foundations, which is a comprehensive parenting program. Blueprints gained a reputation for producing transformational change and keeping children in their homes rather than out-of-home placements. Intending to bring these services to even more families, Shane merged with a multisite allied health services agency in Puget Sound in 2015, bringing Blueprints with him to his new partnership. Blueprints expanded its offerings by adding a preschool program, an early intensive behavioral intervention, and psychological services.

With 20 years of specialized experience and expertise in supporting families with children with significant behavioral challenges, Shane now consults with behavioral health agencies to establish/improve and sustain quality clinical practices, systems, and tools.

Missy Sieders, B.A., Parent Advisor at PEAK Parent Training and Information Center in Colorado, Certified Nurse's Aide for daughter who experiences an intellectual disability, Facilitator for Parents Encouraging Parents Conferences by the Colorado Department of Education

Missy is a parent advisor at PEAK Parent Center, consulting with families, service providers, and educators on inclusive education practices for students with disabilities. She designs and delivers online and live training sessions for families and educators in areas such as effective communications and advocacy skills, the Individuals with Disabilities Education Act, accommodations and modifications, developing friendships, and individualized education program (IEP) facilitation. She contributes to the PEAK Parent Center Blog and is a certified IEP facilitator. She is also a Certified Nurse's Aide for her daughter. She was a Colorado Special Education Advisory Committee member for 7 years and has served on numerous advisory committees for the Colorado Department of Education's Exceptional Student Services Unit. Missy graduated with high honors from Michigan State University with a bachelor's degree in industrial engineering. She has completed postgraduate work in the field of human resource development at Webster University.

Foreword

Positive behavior support (PBS) emerged in the late 1980s as a systematic process for developing and implementing research-based procedures for addressing the serious challenging behaviors of individuals (Carr et al., 2002; Horner et al., 1990). PBS was designed as an educative approach that relied on individualized assessment and avoided reliance on aversive techniques. Initially, PBS was intended for use with severe challenging behaviors exhibited by individuals with autism and significant intellectual disabilities; however, the appeal of PBS soon led to applications with much broader populations. In only a few years, PBS was adopted for use with behavior disorders, in early childhood classrooms, and even with children and youth who displayed problem behaviors but had no associated disability labels. Individualized PBS applications were employed in schools, communities, and family residences.

It soon became apparent that the effectiveness of individualized PBS was dependent to a large extent on the quality of the environmental context in which the process was implemented. And, so, efforts began to focus on larger units of analysis, such as whole classrooms and schools. Schoolwide positive behavior support (or positive behavior interventions and supports; PBIS) was developed in order to establish school cultures that promote adaptive, prosocial behavior and prevent disruptive, challenging behavior (Sugai et al., 2000). The multi-tiered system of support that characterizes schoolwide PBS was then tailored to meet the needs of early childhood programs including preschool classrooms, child care centers, and Head Start (Fox et al., 2003). It soon became apparent that these school and programwide strategies, when implemented effectively, could prevent the occurrence of many disruptive behaviors and, in some cases, obviate the need for individualized PBS altogether.

Let us now consider challenging behaviors in the context of families and home settings. There have been efforts to implement individualized PBS with families for more than 25 years, and some of these efforts produced satisfying outcomes (e.g., Durand et al., 2013; Lucyshyn et al., 2002; Vaughn et al., 1997). Resource manuals and books describing strategies for using PBS in homes and communities were produced. The most valuable of these resources was authored by Meme Hieneman, Karen Childs (Elfer), and Jane Sergay in 2006. As far as I know, it was the only authoritative resource that was written for parents as a guide for parents to use in implementing the process of individualized PBS with their own child. While adhering to the research-based principles and process of PBS, the book was a detailed, reader-friendly guide for implementation of effective support. I am happy to report that this book is now in an upgraded second edition and available as *Resolving Your Child's Challenging Behavior: A Practical Guide to Parenting With Positive Behavior Support* (Hieneman, Elfner, & Sergay, 2022).

There is a problem—a significant limitation—in implementing PBS with families. The problem is analogous to the problem we encountered in using individualized PBS in classrooms. That is, if the context, the school or family culture, is not conducive to the right kind of change, then there is little likelihood that PBS will be implemented with integrity, sustainability, or effectiveness. If there is an absence of organization, clear expectations, and sensible routines, then PBS is likely to fail. I encounter this issue very often in the work that we do with families (Dunlap et al., 2017). Our answer to this frustration has been to recommend a set of foundational practices (structured routines, clear behavioral expectations, high rates of praise, etc.) prior to the PBS process, and sometimes this works pretty well. Indeed, there have been many occasions when the introduction of these foundational practices has served to fully resolve the "serious" problems that led to a referral for intensive and effortful PBS. However, sometimes these simple recommendations are not nearly enough.

It seems as if a more comprehensive solution would be to create a "familywide PBS" process, in a manner similar to what we have in place with schoolwide and programwide PBS. After all, much has been studied and written about family systems, and many recommendations have been put forth, but to my knowledge, there have been no books that have described family-systems process in the framework of PBS. Until now.

Meme Hieneman and her coauthors, Sarah Fefer, Shane Isley, and Missy Sieders, have provided a groundbreaking, user-friendly guidebook for families that articulates a solid process through which families can enhance and improve the ways that they solve problems and learn to interact more pleasantly and constructively. It is the book is in your hands: *Helping Your Family Thrive: A Practical Guide to Parenting With Positive Behavior Support*. The process described in the book will be familiar to PBSers. There are a) a series of assessments, including a Family PBS Self-Check, b) goal-setting involving creating a family vision and expectations, c) making arrangements in the family environment, d) teaching behavior expectations and, of course, e) monitoring outcomes and problem solving. Movement through this process is facilitated by rich examples, a downloadable workbook, and case illustrations.

I used a few adjectives to describe this book, and I should explain them. It is "user-friendly" because it was written with parents as the primary consumer. The text avoids jargon and presents the PBS process in clear, linear, and straightforward language. The book is "groundbreaking" because it is the first systematic effort to bring PBS principles to the behavior of family systems. I believe that this book will be the first of many, and that future efforts in family support will use this model as the starting point. I also believe that the book will inspire research, and I hope it does. Although I have confidence that the model will be effective, its real value and potential will come from an empirical foundation. That is something to which I can look forward. In the meantime, this is a model and a process that I will strongly recommend. It has the power to help families in truly meaningful ways.

I wish to close this foreword with a word of thanks to the authors. This is an innovative and practical guide, and I sincerely appreciate its availability, but I must also issue a note of great sadness. The lead author of this book, and our good friend,

Meme Hieneman, died in August of 2021, following a lengthy struggle with cancer. Meme was a talented and generous woman who lived her life with courage and grace and humanity. I had known Meme for several decades, and I had the privilege of serving as her doctoral advisor at the University of South Florida. Meme made numerous contributions to the development and dissemination of PBS. This book is a wonderful example and a meaningful tribute. We will miss Meme greatly.

Glen Dunlap, Ph.D.
University of Nevada, Reno

REFERENCES

Carr, E. G., Dunlap, G., Horner, R. H., Koegel, R. L., Turnbull, A. P., Sailor, W., Anderson, J., Albin, R.W., Koegel, L. K., & Fox, L. (2002). Positive behavior support. Evolution of an applied science. *Journal of Positive Behavior Interventions, 4*, 4–16.

Dunlap, G., Strain, P., Lee, J. K., Joseph, J., Vatland, C., & Fox, L. (2017). *Prevent-Teach-Reinforce for Families: A model of individualized positive behavior support for home and community.* Paul H. Brookes Publishing Co.

Durand, V. M., Hieneman, M., Clarke, S., Wang, M., & Rinaldi, M. (2013). Positive family intervention for severe challenging behavior I: A multi-site randomized clinical trial. *Journal of Positive Behavior Interventions, 15*, 133–143.

Fox, L., Dunlap, G., Hemmeter, M. L., Joseph, G. E., & Strain, P. S. (2003). The teaching pyramid: A model for supporting social competence and preventing challenging behavior in young children. *Young Children, July 2003*, 48–52.

Hieneman, M., Childs, K., & Sergay, J. (2006). *Parenting with positive behavior support: A practical guide to resolving your child's difficult behavior.* Paul H. Brookes Publishing Co.

Hieneman, M., Elfner, K., & Sergay, J. (2022). *Resolving your child's challenging behavior: A practical guide to parenting with positive behavior support* (2nd ed.). Paul H. Brookes Publishing Co.

Horner, R. H., Dunlap, G., Koegel, R. L., Carr, E. G., Sailor, W., Anderson, J., Albin, R. W., & O'Neill, R. E. (1990). In support of integration for people with severe problem behaviors: A response to four commentaries. *Journal of the Association for Persons with Severe Handicaps, 15*, 145–147.

Lucyshyn, J., Dunlap, G., & Albin, R. W. (Eds.) (2002). *Families and positive behavior support: Addressing problem behaviors in family contexts.* Paul H. Brookes Publishing Co.

Sugai, G., Horner, R. H., Dunlap, G., Hieneman, M., Lewis, T. J., Nelson, C. M., Scott, T., Liaupsin, C., Sailor, W., Turnbull, A. P., Turnbull, H. R. III, Wickham, D., Ruef, M., & Wilcox, B. (2000). Applying positive behavior support and functional behavioral assessment in schools. *Journal of Positive Behavior Interventions, 2*, 131–143.

Vaughn, B. J., Dunlap, G., Fox, L., Clarke, S., & Bucy, M. (1997). Parent-professional partnership in behavioral support: A case study of community-based intervention. *Journal of the Association for Persons with Severe Handicaps, 22*, 185–197.

Note to the Reader

This book is written especially for you, the parent, caregiver, or other family member who would like to enhance your family functioning to produce the best possible behavior in your children while helping them grow socially and emotionally. *Helping Your Family Thrive: A Practical Guide to Parenting With Positive Behavior Support* will help you assess and enhance your current approach to supporting your children's behavior using a proactive, problem-solving process called *positive behavior support (PBS)*.

WHY DID WE WRITE THIS BOOK?

Throughout our careers and personal lives, we have witnessed the potential of PBS and recognized its benefits for families. Meme started on this journey when her children were still infants, writing a book with her colleagues Karen Elfner and Jane Sergay titled *Parenting With Positive Behavior Support: A Practical Guide to Resolving Your Child's Difficult Behavior* (2006), now in its second edition as *Resolving Your Child's Challenging Behavior: A Practical Guide to Parenting With Positive Behavior Support* (2022). Meme and her colleagues designed that book for parents who were facing behavioral challenges with their kids. It was helpful for many, but it did not apply to typical families who simply wanted to organize their lives to promote the best possible behavior in their children or get out in front of problems. Employing the principles and processes of PBS allows families to clarify expectations, set the stage for desired behavior by organizing their social and physical environments, and effectively respond to children's behavior.

PBS has been used to support individual children within families and has been adopted broadly in schools (i.e., positive behavior interventions and supports or PBIS) to improve their systemwide discipline practices. Not much has been written regarding how PBS can be applied within entire family systems. And much of what has been written includes technical jargon that makes the approach hard to digest for ordinary families. A variety of books are available that provide guidance for behavioral support in families, but few of them offer 1) a pragmatic, family-friendly, problem-solving approach that may be individualized to any situation and 2) a strong research basis to support the principles, processes, and practices. This book provides the guidance you need to strengthen the desired behavior in your household and improve your quality of life.

Helping Your Family Thrive and *Resolving Your Child's Challenging Behavior* are complementary. One book helps families apply PBS holistically to improve family life overall; the other helps families use PBS to address specific challenges. *Helping Your Family Thrive* is about prevention and focuses on the whole family and home environment, whereas the other book is about responding when challenging behaviors occur. Both books guide readers through a PBS process that involves identifying goals, analyzing behavior patterns, designing strategies, using your plan, and monitoring progress—a continuing cycle as your family changes over time (see Figure I.1.) Each book stands alone; however, readers are also encouraged to use them together, starting with the book that aligns with their immediate needs.

A robust research basis supports the problem-solving approach, principles, and practices described in this book. Furthermore, the approach has been practiced with close to 150 individual families of neurodiverse children with significant behavioral challenges as part of a family-centered PBS program in Seattle, Washington. Dr. Hieneman and Shane Isley (Blueprints founder) collaborated to design and support the implementation of a family systems PBS model (Blueprints Family Systems Model) that used evidence-based practices (e.g., functional behavior assessments, positive behavioral interventions, measurement systems) to target four critical areas of family functioning: 1) structural, 2) interactional, 3) ecological, and 4) cognitive-emotive. The Blueprints program helped families

- Refine their household structure (e.g., household arrangement, scheduling, expectations)

- Increase and support behaviors that result in positive interactions within families (e.g., communication, consistency)

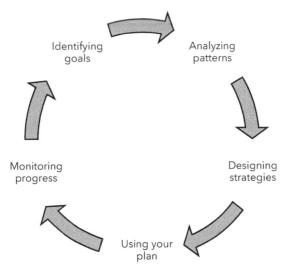

Figure I.1. The cycle of the positive behavior support process. (From Hieneman, M., Raulston, T., & Strobel, L. [2017]. *Special issue: Positive behavior support in family routines* [six-article series]. *Parenting Special Needs* magazine [online]. https://magazine.parentingspecialneeds.org/publication/?m=13847&i=461820&p=1&ver =html5)

- Enhance family ecology (e.g., broaden social networks and community participation)

- Address the cognitive and emotional barriers that make parenting challenging (e.g., optimism, buy-in, parental efficacy)

This family-centered approach produced socially valid and statistically significant outcomes for families of children with challenging behaviors. In some cases, we observed transformational change for individuals with challenges and their families.

FOR WHOM IS THE BOOK INTENDED?

This book is intended for parents and other primary caregivers who want to approach their children's behavior proactively, positively, and functionally (i.e., in ways that work). Please note that we use a broad definition of *parents* to include stepparents, grandparents, adoptive and foster parents, and kinship relationships, as well as biological parents. This book may also be beneficial for other family members to promote consistency in everyone's approach. In addition, we expect that therapists, behavior analysts, counselors, teachers, parent educators, and other professionals will find this book to be a good resource in their support of families. This book's organization, examples, and activities are also well suited for parent education programs.

Similarly, we use the terms *home* and *household* broadly to refer to the family's shared living space, whether this is a house, an apartment, an arrangement to stay with someone outside of the immediate family or in a motel or shelter, or any other shared family space, temporary or permanent. Regardless of immediate circumstances, all families can consider their home environment in supporting their family's quality of life.

HOW IS THIS BOOK ORGANIZED?

Helping Your Family Thrive is divided into three sections. Section I introduces the principles of PBS, explains how a family functions as a system, and gives an overview of how PBS can be used to improve family life. Section II offers a step-by-step process for strengthening your family so you can all thrive. Section III provides further recommendations for enhancing family functioning and shares stories of how two specific families followed the PBS process. Each section includes a variety of examples and practice activities to reinforce the information provided.

This book is accompanied by online resources to support families in using PBS. The *Helping Your Family Thrive* workbook is available on the Brookes Download Hub, along with an Excel spreadsheet for monitoring progress. The workbook consists of fillable PDF forms for completing a family self-assessment and developing a Family PBS Plan. You may choose to download the full workbook or download each form individually when you need it. See the Downloadable Resources lists throughout the book to identify what you will need for a given chapter.

HOW SHOULD THE BOOK BE USED?

This book outlines a problem-solving process and a set of principles that should be applied in an individualized manner. It is not a program or a set of practices, but instead is a framework for decision making that allows families to create their own solutions. Although we offer lots of examples, we expect our readers to use their creativity and problem-solving abilities, relying on the book as a guide. To get the most out of this book, we encourage the following.

- *Apply what you learn.* Work through the exercises and forms as you read. Use the various activities, Before You Move On reminders and What Do You Think? exercises, to apply PBS to the case examples as well as to your own family. Record your thoughts and notes directly in the book, in a separate notebook or file, and/or in the downloadable forms. (Access to those supporting resources is available through the Brookes Download Hub; see the About the Downloads page.) There is no one correct way to work through the book as long as you are actively engaging with the content and applying what you learn to your own family.

- *Be creative.* Do not adopt the practices unless they really fit your situation.

- *Work collaboratively.* Engage other caregivers and your children in the process.

- *Integrate other approaches.* If you already do things that work and align with the general principles in the book, then keep doing them.

- *Track progress.* Monitor how your family is doing and make periodic adjustments when needed to ensure that the plan is doable and beneficial.

Thank you for picking up this book. We hope PBS is as helpful for your family as it has been for ours.

Acknowledgments

This book is based not only on our own personal and professional experiences but also on our colleagues and friends. We have benefited from amazing research in both PBS and parenting (see the Resources list at the end of the book). We have learned the most from the families with whom we have interacted over the years. They have shared their challenges and triumphs, and their stories have helped shape the contents of this book. Thank you to all of our teachers.

We are thankful for the competent and supportive staff at Paul H. Brookes Publishing Co., who kept our vision for the complementary two-book concept alive and helped to make it a reality.

And finally, we would like to thank our families and friends for their continued encouragement and support.

In Memoriam

MARY ELLEN (MEME) HIENEMAN (1965-2021)

Our inspiring friend and colleague, Dr. Meme Hieneman, lost her long, courageous struggle with cancer before the second edition of *Resolving Your Child's Challenging Behavior* was published. Thankfully, and somewhat astonishingly, given her diminishing physical condition, she was able to orchestrate the revisions to the original text and to realize her vision of publishing a companion book, *Helping Your Family Thrive*, before she passed. Meme was determined to share her passion for family-based positive behavior supports with the world, and she set her sights on completing both texts as one of her final missions.

Meme left a devoted family, colleagues, students, and countless individuals who were recipients of her commitment to individuals with significant behavioral challenges and their families. Meme's contributions to the field of positive behavior support (PBS) were numerous and wide ranging. She embodied the principles of PBS in everything that she did and worked with many collaborators to ensure that her influence on the field will persist. Her legacy includes many articles for *Parenting Special Needs* magazine, creation of the Home and Community Positive Behavior Support Network, development of the *Practiced Routines* curriculum, numerous innovative and influential research projects, and much more.

Whether conducting research and writing, consulting, teaching, or advocating, Meme was tireless in her resolve to extend the effective use of positive behavior support technologies in home and community settings. She was brilliant, bold, and tenacious, just the kind of supporter you would want in your corner. You will see this spirit throughout both *Resolving Your Child's Challenging Behavior* and *Helping Your Family Thrive*. Meme's legacy lives on in the individuals who continue to be influenced by the organizations she originated, the influential mentoring and coaching provided, and the valuable resources left for all to access.

Introduction and Overview

Positive Behavior Support for Families

Section I of this book introduces you to positive behavior support. In Chapter 1, we explain its basic principles and approaches as a foundation for supporting or improving the day-to-day behavior of your entire family. In Chapter 2, we discuss how this approach applies to families, with a special consideration of the unique variations in family compositions, values, perspectives, dynamics, and needs.

1

Introducing Positive Behavior Support

Positive behavior support (PBS) is a practical, research-based approach for supporting people's behavior within their typical daily routines and settings. It was originally defined as an approach for addressing behavioral challenges of people with disabilities that combined the principles of applied behavior analysis (ABA) with person and family-centered values. As PBS has evolved, it has expanded its focus to include people with other behavioral support needs and demonstrated its effectiveness when applied to entire systems. This chapter introduces the core features of PBS. It will clarify that no one size fits all; strategies must be tied to the unique characteristics, needs, and behavior patterns of each individual person and family.

BACKGROUND AND RATIONALE FOR POSITIVE BEHAVIOR SUPPORT

Historically, our society has often been reactive and punitive when addressing behavior. There was a common perspective that if one "spares the rod, they spoil the child" and a tendency to correct or respond to misbehavior, rather than teach new skills. We have increasingly come to understand that we can support behavior more effectively if we understand its purposes and develop strategies to get out in front of problems. We recognize that challenging behavior often occurs because people do not have better ways of handling their circumstances. Finally, we recognize that the way we respond or react to behavior affects whether the behavior will continue or even escalate. These are the core principles of ABA, which is the technical foundation for PBS (Dunlap & Horner, 2006).

Another important evolution has occurred in our approach to behavior. We used to see behavior only at the level of the individual person, not recognizing that behavior is influenced by what other people in the environment say and do. This ecological (i.e., big picture) perspective is very important because groups, systems, and communities all have an impact on people's behavior. It is helpful to look more broadly at behavior within settings (e.g., classrooms, schools, organizations)—and that includes families. PBS offers this ecological, proactive perspective and recognizes that it is essential to engage all family members to ensure that behavior support strategies fit their needs and circumstances and will promote positive and productive family functioning. Each of these elements of PBS are described next.

ELEMENTS OF EFFECTIVE SUPPORT

PBS is a process and set of principles to guide planning and decision making, rather than rigid procedures. Given this, PBS can be tailored to essentially any situation by ensuring that plans are based on a complete understanding of the home and community environment and family preferences, needs, and patterns of behavior. Professionals may be able to support families in this process, but the ownership must remain with the families themselves, engaging all members in the decision-making process. PBS plans are not single-strategy quick fixes, but instead a comprehensive approach that involves proactive strategies, teaching skills, and managing consequences, as well as broader support to improve family life.

Core elements of effective support include

- Understanding behavior, including the context in which it occurs and the purpose(s) it serves for the individual

- Developing comprehensive support plans that include proactive, teaching, and management strategies

- Improving lives by not only addressing challenges but also helping families thrive overall

These elements are discussed in the following sections.

Understanding Behavior

One of the grounding principles of PBS is that people respond in unique ways to environmental circumstances and are driven to achieve different outcomes. For this reason, we begin our process by gaining an understanding of the needs of everyone involved and the patterns contributing to desired and challenging behavior. We do this with the A-B-C (antecedent-behavior-consequence) model.

Antecedents, Behavior, and Consequences   *Behavior* is what people say or do. We try to look at behavior as objectively as possible because assumptions can cloud our judgments. For example, rather than labeling a behavior as aggressive, we would simply say that a child hit or yelled at her sibling. *Antecedents* refer to events or conditions that come before behavior and may include interactions with other people (e.g., being asked to do something, told no, or ignored) or environmental changes (e.g., changes in setting or schedules). They may also include broader issues (sometimes called *setting events*) such as historical events, illness, ongoing conflict, or changes in routines. For example, if we are under a lot of stress at work and find that our child skipped school or got into a fight, we may be more likely to overreact. The COVID-19 pandemic is another example of a setting event that had a large impact on family dynamics and behavior for many. Finally, *consequences* are the reactions or results that occur following the behavior. People commonly get or avoid things through their behavior. Desirable consequences tend to increase behavior, whereas undesirable consequences tend to decrease behavior. Consequences may be planned or incidental, but regardless of which they are, they affect the likelihood of the behavior happening in the future.

Purposes of Behavior Behavior has four primary purposes. These purposes (or in technical ABA language, "functions") relate to desirable and challenging behavior. First, behavior can be motivated by attention. A parent may say "excuse me"—or yell loudly—to get their child to listen. Second, behavior may occur to gain access to items or activities. A child may request or grab items off the shelves in the grocery store or demand to play video games. Third, behavior may be driven by avoiding or stopping an unpleasant event. A parent may give in to a child's demands for items or activities because they are worn down by nagging. Giving in often causes the child's challenging behavior to stop, at least for the time being. Finally, behavior can have a self-stimulatory function, which means the activity itself is pleasurable and no social contingencies are in play. Many of us enjoy binge-watching certain programs, playing video games, exercising vigorously, or engaging in other activities that provide stimulation.

Behavior can also serve more than one function or result in complex outcomes. For example, a child might be sent to their room because they talk back to a parent. If a parent provides attention while arguing with the child about their behavior, and the child gets to read comic books in the room, then multiple reinforcing outcomes may be in play. Gaining or regaining control of circumstances can also be a powerful outcome of behavior. For example, this might occur when a parent yells at her children until they finally do what they are told or a child turns the tables on a parent during an argument so that the parent gives in. Understanding the different purposes that behavior serves and the antecedents that set the stage for the behavior is important in building effective strategies.

Developing Comprehensive Support Plans

Effective PBS strategies are individualized and tailored to the specific patterns maintaining the behavior. Although quick fixes may be popular, we cannot expect that a single strategy (e.g., time-out) will ultimately produce long-term improvements. Instead, we put together comprehensive supports that include implementing proactive and preventive strategies, teaching desired behavior (e.g., to replace challenging behavior), and managing consequences that follow behavior to ensure that we are responding consistently and effectively. Table 1.1 provides a summary of different proactive, teaching, and management strategies tailored to the four functions/purposes of behavior.

Using Proactive Strategies   Proactive strategies involve setting up situations to prompt desired behavior and prevent or minimize problems. Because

Table 1.1.   Function-based interventions

Function or purpose	Proactive strategies	Replacement skills	Management strategies
Gaining attention	Increase the amount of attention provided throughout the day. Let the person know when attention will be available. Provide other activities when busy and unable to interact. Prompt the person to request attention appropriately.	Teach the person to request attention, such as proximity (come here), interaction (talk to me), or physical contact. Teach the person to engage in alternative activities when attention is not available.	Increase level and frequency of desired attention following desired behavior. Minimize attention (e.g., by ignoring, walking away) when challenging behavior occurs.
Obtaining items or activities	Clarify what items and activities are available. Remove off-limits items from the surroundings. Offer alternative activities or items when you must say "no." Prompt the person to request or negotiate alternatives.	Teach the person to request items or activities or initiate access to activities on their own. Teach the person to accept alternative choices, to wait, and to accept "no."	Provide desired items or activities only following appropriate behavior (e.g., requests). Withhold desired items or activities immediately after challenging behavior (including negotiation).
Escaping, avoiding, or delaying tasks or situations	Modify aspects of the settings or activities. Provide the person with choices of activities or their timing. Shorten activities or provide periodic breaks during them. Remind person how to request breaks or delays appropriately.	Teach the person to say "no" or "later," take breaks, or use other ways to escape or delay unpleasant places or activities. Teach the person to cooperate and engage in nonpreferred tasks and activities for periods of time.	Allow breaks, delays, changes in the environment, or reductions in demands for appropriate behavior (e.g., participation). Delay assistance or breaks from tasks until challenging behavior stops and the person cooperates.
Sensory stimulation	Provide activities that produce appropriate sensory stimulation. Block the person's access to inappropriate stimulation. Prompt appropriate forms of stimulation.	Teach the person to obtain sensory input through alternative appropriate actions. Teach the person to tolerate periods of reduced or increased stimulation.	Allow access to items and activities that provide appropriate sensory stimulation. Block the person's access to inappropriate events (e.g., flipping items over and over).

we have identified antecedents, conditions, and environmental events that may affect behavior, we are empowered to set the stage for desirable behavior and make challenging behavior less likely to occur in the first place. Proactive strategies may include organizing our households, planning schedules, and establishing clear expectations. For example, we might make sure that everything children need to complete their homework is stored in one place. We might post a calendar on the refrigerator to include all family activities. We might review expectations for behavior prior to going to a restaurant. More examples of proactive strategies are provided throughout the book.

Teaching Replacement Skills   Teaching skills is very important in PBS because children (and adults) often lack the communication, social, organizational, daily living, problem solving, self-management, or other skills to effectively negotiate their circumstances. We must avoid assuming that family members are simply unmotivated or being uncooperative. Instead, we should determine if they need better ways to get attention, items, or activities they desire or delay or avoid challenging circumstances appropriately (e.g., taking brief breaks, negotiating reductions in demands). We also need to consider if they need skills to effectively participate in social situations, complete tasks expected of them, or simply tolerate frustration. Teaching skills through explaining, modeling, and rewarding performance is critical to long-term success.

Managing Consequences   Managing consequences means that we pay attention to the way we react or respond to behavior. Our goal is to maximize reinforcement (e.g., access to attention, special privileges or items, preferred activities, opportunities to avoid tasks) for desired behavior and minimize reinforcement following challenging behavior. For example, if we give our kids a lot of positive attention when they are participating in family activities but ignore their grousing, then they may be more likely to stay engaged. If we provide an allowance or access to screen time after children complete their homework and chores each week, then they may be more cooperative. If we help children with difficult tasks when they are clearly trying or asking for help, then we are reinforcing those efforts. Consequences pertain to parents as well. We should reward ourselves for being proactive and staying even keeled during family interactions (e.g., with a piece of chocolate, a long bath, or watching our favorite show).

Improving Lives

PBS is not only about motivating and managing behavior, it is also about creating the best possible lives for families. This often involves broadening our focus to other areas that affect families, such as work and home demands, interpersonal relationships, physical and mental health, communication, schedules and routines, household structure, and available support systems. These factors are certain to affect family functioning and enjoyment; therefore, it is necessary to look beyond the moment-to-moment interactions to long-term considerations and the big picture. For example, if all family members are not communicating openly and effectively, then it is very difficult to resolve problems. If histories of trauma are affecting family members' reactions to situations, then they cannot be ignored. If the demands on family members' time are overwhelming, then it may feel next to impossible to shift to a more proactive, planful approach. For this reason, it may be important to ensure that the timing of initiating and engaging in the family-focused process described in this book works for everyone involved. Therefore, it is critical that PBS is viewed as a collaborative process in which parents and children work together to build on the family's strengths, take advantage of available resources, identify and resolve problems, and strengthen their connections with each other.

SUMMARY: WHAT IS POSITIVE BEHAVIOR SUPPORT?

PBS has been applied successfully across various people and settings and aligns with recommended best practices (e.g., American Academy of Pediatrics). PBS focuses on 1) understanding why behavior occurs and continues to occur, 2) developing comprehensive, individualized strategies to prevent, teach, and reinforce behavior, and 3) improving the lives of all involved.

BEFORE MOVING ON

- Do you understand the role PBS can play in improving the lives of individuals and families so they can thrive?

- Are you able to describe and provide examples of the key features of PBS?

Understanding Family Systems

Strong families are essential to child development. They provide a critical foundation for children to learn to care for themselves and their surroundings, develop and maintain healthy relationships, and successfully participate in society. Families can provide a safe haven for their members in this chaotic world. When families struggle, every member is affected. Dysfunctional family behavior, chaotic household environments, or a lack of clarity and consistency in expectations can lead to emotional problems and challenging behavior. For these reasons, strengthening family units and creating supportive home environments is an essential goal in our society.

FAMILY CHARACTERISTICS

All families are unique and vary significantly in their composition, characteristics, and preferences. Since the 1960s, the number of two-parent families has dropped from 73% to 46% (Pew Research Center, 2015). More households are managed by single parents, more parents are cohabitating, and more children make the transition between multiple homes. About 15% of children under the age of 18 are living with people other than their biological parents, including stepparents, adoptive or foster families, grandparents, and other kin. The number of families in which both parents work outside the home is very high, often making it necessary to coordinate parenting with extended family members or other child care providers. Families may be blended and multigenerational, with members embracing different core values, expectations, decision-making processes, discipline methods, and routines. Throughout this book, we use the terms *home* and *household* generally to apply to these different family arrangements. Although we frequently refer to *parents*, the guidance we provide is equally appropriate for any adult who is responsible for managing a household, providing care to other members of that household, and supporting their family's well-being.

Families vary significantly in their cultural and religious perspectives, which affect their approach to parenting. Families may have particular traditions or values that guide how they interact. The life stage of the family is also important because practices need to evolve as parents and children get older. Many families are burdened by challenges. Money might be tight. Parents may be supporting a family member with a disability or serious illness as well as caring for their own children. Members of families may have experienced trauma (e.g., neglect, abuse, abandonment) that continues to affect their trust and responses to seemingly common events. Relationships among family members—marital, sibling, parental, extended family—may be strained, leading to inconsistent, reactive, or unproductive family interactions. Family members may be struggling with substance abuse or living in unsafe communities.

Yet, all families have strengths. Members may pull together in times of crisis, support one another's accomplishments, or overcome challenges. All of these variables are important to consider in tailoring the PBS process to family needs.

Meet the Wagner Family

To illustrate PBS in family life, we will introduce you to the Wagner family. Josef and Sara are married with four children—Thom (16), Shannon (13), Julia (10), and Tristan (3). They live in an older, middle-class home, which is comfortable but requires a lot of maintenance. Josef works as a city planner. His work requires some meetings in the evenings and periodic in-state travel. Sara is a nurse and typically works 12-hour shifts Monday through Wednesdays. This is Josef's second marriage and Sara's first.

Thom has his driver's license, plays drums in the high school marching band, and is trying to start a band with some friends. Shannon plays soccer and is involved in theater at middle school. She is trying to start a dog-walking and pet-sitting business in the neighborhood. Julia loves listening to music, going to live theater plays, and watching Disney movies. She has a reading disability, speech delay, and is sensitive to bright lights, loud sounds, and tight crowds. Therefore, in addition to coordinating with all of the children's teachers, the band director, and coaches, the parents must ensure that Julia is receiving appropriate educational and therapy services. Tristan loves playing with cars and being read to by anyone who will sit with him. He attends preschool part time.

The Wagner family is fortunate to live near their extended family who assist them with child care and transportation. Their extended family includes Sara's parents (Rob and Joan), Josef's brother, Reuben, and his wife, Melanie, who have two boys of similar ages. Josef's first wife, Kat, works as a bank teller and lives with her long-term boyfriend, David, in the same community. Thom alternates weeks between the two families.

Although things were manageable when the kids were younger, the Wagners experienced new challenges. The parents' jobs were more demanding, Julia was struggling in school, and the older children were pushing for more freedom and focused more on their friends and activities. Whereas family time used to be more fun, routines had become more chaotic and family members felt disconnected and stressed. Luckily, after sharing their recent concerns, Melanie (Josef's and Sara's sister-in-law), who had experience with PBS, shared the process and this book with the family. Although the Wagners understood that it would require a good bit of work, they were hopeful that they would be able to regain their sense of connectedness and enjoyment.

A summary chart for Strengths and Challenges is included with the *Helping Your Family Thrive* workbook. Visit the Brookes Download Hub to obtain a copy—or start by jotting notes on a separate sheet of paper or in the following space. The Wagners' chart is shown in Figure 2.1.

■ ACTIVITY ■ Our Family Strengths and Challenges

Describe the members of your family, your strengths (e.g., resources, sources of support), and current challenges. Include anything that makes your family unique and could affect your approach to parenting and supporting all family members.

The _____ Family

Members

_____   _____
_____
_____

Strengths

_____
_____
_____
_____
_____
_____

Challenges

_____

_____

_____

_____

_____

_____

_____

Wagner Family

Members: *Josef (Dad), Sara (Mom), Thom (16), Shannon (13), Julia (10), and Tristan (3)*

Strengths	Challenges
• We love and enjoy our time together.	• Demands on everyone's time (work hours, kids' activities) leave less time for fun.
• Dad and Mom have good jobs.	• Lots of work is needed to maintain the house.
• We have a comfortable home.	• Growing children are pushing for independence.
• We live within our means.	
• We have good health insurance.	• Julia has a reading disability and speech delay, making school difficult for her.
• Kids' schools and teachers are family friendly.	
• Speech services are offered at home for Julia.	• Josef's Mom is older and has health issues.
• Extended family live nearby and assist with child care when needed.	• Thom splits his time between homes.
• Melanie (sister-in-law) knows positive behavior support.	• Family dinners and transitions (getting ready for school) can be chaotic.
	• Communication breakdowns are occurring.

Figure 2.1.   The Wagner family's Strengths and Challenges worksheet.

EFFECTIVE PARENTING PRACTICES

Four features have been consistently associated with strong families, regardless of the diversity in family characteristics. First, strong families establish clear and consistent values and expectations. They know what they stand for and what behavior is acceptable and not acceptable. Second, strong families emphasize maintaining relationships, putting them above their other priorities. Third, strong families provide appropriate monitoring and supervision for their children. They know where their children are, what they are doing, and with whom they are spending time. Finally, strong families rely on positive discipline methods. The American Academy of Pediatrics (Sege & Siegel, 2018) came out strongly in support of these features and emphasized rewarding desirable behavior and avoiding harsh punishments. Evidence-based parenting programs such as Incredible Years and the Positive Parenting Program include these features as well (see Hieneman & Fefer, 2017).

Given the diversity in the circumstances and needs of families, a one-size-fits-all approach does not make sense. Basic principles of parenting and family management may be applied differently based on family characteristics, values, and preferences. It is critical that family members are able to communicate openly and respectfully with one another to effectively embark on a family strengthening process. This means resolving conflicts and problems together. They must also make positive family interactions a priority, committing the necessary time and energy to the process. If these things seem difficult, then it may be necessary to seek professional help or address important barriers before beginning. Chapter 8 of this book may also be helpful.

ABOUT USING THIS BOOK

This book is designed to provide an individualized problem solving and family strengthening guide for families. It is, in essence, a workbook for your family. Section I has introduced you to the elements of PBS and family systems. Now you're ready to move on to the heart of the book—Section II, which guides you through five steps to use PBS to help your family thrive.

The first step is family self-assessment to determine what practices you currently have in place and what gaps may exist. We provide monitoring tools to assist you in problem solving and tracking your progress. You then proceed chapter by chapter to

- Clarify your family vision and expectations.

- Consider how you might structure your household space and schedules to better support desirable behavior.

- Teach behavioral expectations. To do so, you will need to identify and teach skills family members need to participate more fully in daily routines, interact more positively, and overcome problems and also determine effective ways to respond to behavior (focusing on reinforcing desired behavior).

• Continuously monitor how your family is doing and address challenges that may arise.

You will have activities to complete in each chapter to help you apply what you are learning within your family. The final section of this book covers processes to help sustain the progress your family achieves and provides case examples of family support plans. Please note that these examples are simply illustrative. You should create your own solutions and strategies based on the principles and practices you learn through the process.

We strongly recommend you work through this process with your family, ensuring that everyone has input during each of the activities. By doing so, you will ensure the entire family has ownership and investment in the plan that is developed. You may find it helpful to revisit chapters of this book and aspects of your family plan as your children mature and things change in your life. All of the activities are included as blank forms within the downloadable resources accompanying the book. Other resources are included at the back of the book if you want to explore any of the topics in greater depth.

SUMMARY: HOW CAN OUR FAMILY USE POSITIVE BEHAVIOR SUPPORT?

Families are unique in terms of their composition, strengths, characteristics, and needs. The process and approaches in this book should be tailored to each individual family. As can be seen in the case studies included within this book, each family will use the PBS process differently and prioritize the steps that will best support their family's current needs. Some families may include teachers, pediatricians, or service providers on their team to implement PBS. Some families may have special considerations for family members with disabilities or related to changes in family composition, such as a new infant, a divorce, or an older family member moving in the house. The approach outlined here is flexible, and families may choose to focus on specific components that fit best with their context in order to help all family members thrive.

BEFORE MOVING ON

• Have you identified your family's important strengths and challenges?

• How will you continue to focus on these issues as you proceed through the book?

Five Steps to Help Your Family Thrive

Using Positive Behavior Support

Section I provided an introduction to help you understand PBS and family systems. PBS is not a one size fits-all approach. Rather, it is a process you can tailor to your family's individual characteristics, goals, and needs.

The companion volume to this book, *Resolving Your Child's Challenging Behavior: A Practical Guide to Parenting With Positive Behavior Support* (Hieneman et al., 2022), describes how to apply PBS principles to address situations in which one child's challenging behavior negatively affects the family's functioning (e.g., refusing to stay in bed at night and thus disrupting everyone's sleep). These principles include understanding behavior, improving lives, working together, and using multi-element plans that include promoting positive behavior, preventing difficult situations, teaching, and management. In this book, we explain how to apply the same PBS principles more holistically to improve overall family quality of life. This approach is proactive and focused on preventing further challenges, rather than in response to identified problems. Section II guides you to define what optimal functioning means for your family, identify circumstances that may be getting in the way of that, and prioritize and address needed changes. Chapters 3–7 describe each step in the process:

1. Assessing existing behavior patterns and supports

2. Creating your vision and expectations

3. Organizing your physical space and time

4. Teaching behavioral expectations

5. Monitoring results and solving any problems that arise

To illustrate the entire process, step by step, we continue to follow the Wagners, the example family introduced in Section I. Their four children's ages range from the preschool years through the teens, and each child has unique strengths, interests, and challenges, as do the adults. The detailed examples of how the Wagner family applies PBS aim to show how the process can be used to help a whole family thrive—individually and together.

3

Completing a Family Self-Assessment

It is helpful to do some self-assessment before launching into the development of a comprehensive plan for supporting your family. This includes determining how your family is currently functioning and what effective supports you already have in place. In this chapter, we help guide you to complete two different self-assessments. The first has two parts: 1) a Weekly Family Behavior Rating Tool to help you better determine when you are making progress toward your goals and when it's time to make a change and 2) a Family Interaction Journal to track positive and negative interactions and identify the circumstances surrounding each type of interaction. You can identify patterns in current family behavior by using the rating tool and journal. The second is a Family PBS Self-Check, which is a tool to determine what practical PBS strategies you already have in place and what pieces might be missing. This information will help you focus on the most important topics in the following chapters.

IDENTIFYING CURRENT FAMILY BEHAVIOR PATTERNS

The Weekly Family Behavior Rating Tool lists descriptions of several positive family behaviors related to treating others respectfully and being responsible. The family works together to determine a rating for each behavior based on how consistently family members demonstrate this behavior (0 = never or rarely, 1 = sometimes, 2 = usually, and 3 = always). This tool is useful to help understand current family functioning, make decisions about specific areas to prioritize, and determine if positive changes are occurring over time.

The Wagner Family: Identifying Behavior Patterns

The parents and three older children completed their initial family behavior rating together, discussing each item and coming to a consensus. Tristan did not participate but instead watched a movie. The ratings that Josef, Sara, Thom, Shannon, and Julia agreed to are shown in Figure 3.1. They rated their family

Weekly Family Behavior Rating: *Wagner Family*				
	Never/ rarely	Sometimes	Usually	Always
Family members complete their assigned chores (and homework) completely and correctly.	(0)	1	2	3
Family members listen and respond to instructions without delay or argument.	0	(1)	2	3
Family members respect one another's personal space and belongings.	0	1	(2)	3
Family members speak nicely and calmly with one another (e.g., no insults, name calling).	0	1	(2)	3
Family members use gentle hands when interacting (i.e., no physical aggression).	0	1	2	(3)
Family members respect time lines, curfews, and other established limits.	0	(1)	2	3

Figure 3.1.   The Wagners' Weekly Family Behavior Rating Tool.

high in their gentleness with one another. This had always been an expectation in their household, and although Tristan sometimes threw things, that behavior was likely not deliberate and not unusual at his age. They also scored relatively high in respecting personal space and belongings and speaking nicely and calmly with one another. The children have their own bedrooms, clothing, and electronics, limiting potential conflicts. Greater challenges occurred in the shared areas—disagreements about sharing access to the bathroom and use of hygiene products, tossing items out of the way when trying to work in common areas, rifling around for clean laundry, and leaving shoes, backpacks, and other belongings intermixed by the back door. Although the Wagners tried to use good manners and express love openly and did not engage in sarcasm or name-calling, they were prone to yelling when under stress. The family rated themselves lower in listening and responding to one another and respecting time lines. They discussed that the older children and adults often were plugged in or distracted and didn't hear one another. Julia and Tristan might have heard others, but not fully understood. Thom had begun testing curfew limits because he wanted to hang out with his band after practice or events. Josef's work schedule had become increasingly demanding following a recent promotion, making it difficult for him to consistently leave on time to pick up the children. The older children were using their devices to surf the Internet or connect with friends more frequently, making them less connected with what was going on at home. The Wagner family's greatest challenge was distributing and completing chores. Although the children completed their homework on time, Julia required a great deal of help, and the two teens were prone to losing their assignments. Sara and Josef realized they were picking up the lion's share of the house and yard work by default, even though the children had the time and ability to pitch in.

A blank, fillable version of the Weekly Family Behavior Rating Tool is available in the *Helping Your Family Thrive* workbook; to obtain a copy, visit the Brookes Download Hub. For each statement, rate the extent to which family members engage in the behavior, ranging from never to always. You may add an item as well if you have a specific behavioral goal for your family. In addition, you may wish to use the Weekly Family Behavior—Progress Monitoring Tool available with the downloadable resources for this chapter. This Excel spreadsheet lets you record the same type of information as the Weekly Family Behavior Rating Tool form; the spreadsheet automatically graphs the data entered each week to show your family's progress. A sample completed tab and graph are provided.

    In addition to the weekly behavior ratings, we encourage you to use the Family Interaction Journal to record your best and worst times as a family. Completing this activity each week helps you identify specific social or environmental variables (e.g., people present, time of day, location, conditions, specific activities) that may be contributing to your family members' behavior and problem-solve changes you could make to address challenging situations or routines.

The Wagner Family: Identifying Best and Worst Family Times

Sara and Josef identified what they viewed as their best and most challenging routines and decided to record what happened during those times. Figure 3.2 includes two interaction journals—one for evenings and another for dinnertime—that illustrate common experiences during those times. The time prior to bed tended to be quiet and calming, with each family member

Wagner **Family Interaction Journal**		
At Our Best: Successful or Enjoyable Activity		
What was happening before and around us (e.g., activity)?	What did we each say or do?	How did everyone react, and what was the result?
It's 8 p.m. and Josef just finished bathing Tristan, reading to him, and tucking him in his bed. He heads into the family room to find Sara before he heads up to see the other kids. Thom is in his room finishing his homework. Josef stops by. Shannon is in her room reading one of the books in the **Twilight** *series. She hears her dad down by Thom's room. Julia is in her bed laughing as she listens to a* **Dork Diaries** *book on her iPad with her headphones on. Josef walks to the door and waves at her.*	*Josef tells Sara he is headed to bed to read after he says goodnight to the kids, Sara is getting ready to do yoga and meditate in the family room. Josef asks Thom how his homework is going and says goodnight. Shannon calls from her room to ask if she can watch the* **Twilight** *movies after she finishes the books. Julia pauses her audiobook and says, "Hi, Dad! This book is so funny! I want Mom to read the next one out loud with me as she will crack up at the drama queen in the book."*	*Sara tells Josef that his plan sounds good and that she will be in there in about an hour. Thom says he is almost done with his homework and is looking forward to reading his book about the origins of hip-hop in America. He responds to Shannon that they will add the* **Twilight** *series to their movie night list so they can check their rating and watch them together. Josef laughs with Julia, saying that Mom will love to read with her. He reminds the kids that he will take them to school in the morning and "Lights out at 9:30." Everyone calls "goodnight" almost simultaneously, and Josef says, "Sweet dreams."*

Figure 3.2.   The Wagners' Family Interaction Journal.

Wagner Family Interaction Journal (continued)

At Our Worst: Challenging or Frustrating Activity		
What was happening before and around us (e.g., activity)	What did we each say or do?	How did everyone react, and what was the result?
Sara has dinner on the table and hollers loudly, "Come and get it while it's hot!" Tristan is playing alone with a toy car on the family room floor. Josef is in the study doing work emails. Shannon is on her cell on Facetime with a girlfriend. Thom is in his room with music blasting from his cell phone. Julia is in the family room listening to an audio book out loud on her iPad.	Sara steps over a myriad of toys, books, electronics, and a basket of unfolded laundry. She scoops Tristan off the family room floor to put him in his booster seat at the table. Josef yells loudly from the study, "I have to finish an email for work. Be there in 10 minutes!" Shannon heads to the table with her call continuing. Tristan throws one of his cars, hitting her in the head. Thom comes jumping down the stairs three at a time with the loud music still going. Julia suddenly curls up in the family room chair, covers her ears with her hands, and starts sobbing, "No!"	When Tristan's flying car hits Shannon in the arm and she yells "Ow! Tristan, you are such a brat!" Sara yells, "No throwing" at Tristan, looks around, and thinks to herself, "This is insane! I have to work a 12-hour shift at the hospital tomorrow, our family dinner is falling apart again, the house is a mess, and Josef is working overtime while I try to hold it all together. There has to be something we can do differently as I can't go on this way!" The food is cold by the time everyone arrives at the dinner table.

doing their own thing, but also interacting with one another in positive ways. Lines of communication were open and everyone seemed to know what was expected of them. Dinnertime was more chaotic, with the family clearly out-of-sync.

Figure 3.2 shows the Wagner family's completed Interaction Journal form. To complete the Interaction Journal, record what was happening at the time. For example, were you having a meal, playing a game, or just hanging out? What was going on around you, and what precipitated your interaction (i.e., antecedents)? Next, record exactly what everyone said or did (i.e., their behavior). For example, maybe the children started fighting over a toy and you yelled at them or perhaps you asked your partner to do the dishes and they surprised you by saying they were already done. Finally, record what happened afterward, including how family members reacted or what results occurred (i.e., consequences). For example, the situation could have been diffused with laughter or if everyone simply left the room. Try to be as objective and clear as possible. When you connect as a family each week, you can review your entries and discuss what happened and what you might do differently going forward.

A blank, fillable version of this form is available with the downloadable *Helping Your Family Thrive* workbook. To get started on the Family Interaction Journal, visit the Brookes Download Hub, or jot down notes in the following space.

■ ACTIVITY ■ Family Interaction Journal

Describe family interactions when you are at your best and worst.

At Our Best: Successful or Enjoyable Activity

What was happening before and around us (e.g., activity)?

_____

_____

_____

_____

_____

_____

What did we each say or do?

_____

_____

_____

_____

_____

How did everyone react and what was the result?

_____

_____

_____

_____

_____

_____

At Our Worst: Challenging or Frustrating Activity

What was happening before and around us (e.g., activity)?

_____

_____

_____

_____

_____

_____

What did we each say or do?

_____

_____

_____

_____

_____

_____

How did everyone react, and what was the result?

_____

_____

_____

_____

_____

_____

ASSESSING BEHAVIOR SUPPORT PRACTICES

Now that you are doing your ongoing information gathering using the Weekly Family Behavior Rating Tool and Family Interaction Journal, we would like you to complete the Family PBS Self-Check. This tool was developed based on an extensive review of existing research and practical experience working with families. The purpose of the self-check is to help you identify what you already do that works, as well as areas you feel need improvement. It includes items related to your vision and behavioral expectations, organization of space (physical arrangement) and time (scheduling, limits, and routines), and pro-active and reinforcement-based strategies, as well as other areas. Each item describes a specific positive support. For each item, the family rates the extent to which this support is present (not at all, somewhat, or very much). The following example describes the process the Wagner family used to complete their Family PBS Self-Check.

The Wagner Family: Completing the Family PBS Self-Check

The family made time to sit together one evening after dinner to complete the Family PBS Self-Check. They first reviewed and discussed all of the defini-tions, explaining items in which any members said they didn't understand or they felt needed more clarification. Tristan sat in his highchair playing while the rest of the family talked so he could at least hear the discussion. Then each family member (other than Tristan) did their own ratings. The family put all of their individual ratings on a single form. If they all agreed, then they circled the final rating. For example, the family members agreed that "not at all" should be selected for Household Responsibilities because the household was in more disarray since Josef was promoted, and there was no clear plan of who should do what, by when. If the item was rated differently by family members, then each shared why they rated the item in that way. After all of the members shared, they discussed their ideas until they came to a consensus. The rules for the discussion were 1) listen to others' perspectives, 2) take responsibility and avoid blaming others, and 3) be willing to tell others as you learn some-thing new about how they are experiencing the item. For example, Thom and Shannon rated Notice of Schedule Changes as "somewhat" because they felt they were not always notifying their parents when they changed locations, resulting in a lack of consistent supervision. Sara, Josef, and Julia rated it as "not at all" because the parents' work schedules often changed, sometimes with lit-tle notice. Julia felt like she was juggled among her parents, the older kids, and extended family with no warning. The entire family decided to move their rating to "not at all" as they realized there was no consistent process for this and it was creating stress and missed or late arrivals at events for everyone. The family cel-ebrated their areas of strength and decided to focus on three areas of concern: Household Responsibilities, a Shared Family Calendar, and Pre-planned Conse-quences. They chose these three areas because they felt they were foundational to making other changes. This discussion took about 90 minutes for the Wagner family because there were five members contributing to the discussion.

Figure 3.3 shows the Wagners' completed Family PBS Self-Check. A blank, fillable version of the Family PBS Self-Check is available with the download-able *Helping Your Family Thrive* workbook. Please visit the Brookes Download Hub to obtain a copy, or complete the following Family PBS Self-Check, work-ing together as a family (e.g., you may each use different color pens to mark your ratings). Figure 3.4 contains definitions and examples for each item to assist you in completing the Family PBS Self-Check.

Wagner Family PBS Self-Check

Family name: *Wagner*   Member(s) responding: *Josef, Sara, Thom, Shannon, and Julia*

Please rate the degree that each the following are in place by checking the appropriate column.

Family Vision and Expectations	Not at all	Somewhat	Very much
Shared values and goals		X	
Clear behavioral expectations		X	
Rules regarding misbehavior		X	
Household responsibilities	X		
Organization of Space and Time	Not at all	Somewhat	Very much
Good household organization	X		
Shared family calendar	X		
Consistent daily routines		X	
Notice of schedule changes	X		
Time limits on activities		X	
Teaching and Basic Discipline	Not at all	Somewhat	Very much
Explaining and modeling		X	
Praise for positive behavior		X	
Privileges linked to behavior		X	
Pre-planned consequences	X		
Respectful discipline methods		X	
Supporting Family Life	Not at all	Somewhat	Very much
Open, clear communication		X	
General respect and kindness		X	
Effective problem resolution	X		
Strong, loving relationships			X
Ability to manage stress		X	
Support of family and friends			X
Full community participation			X

Figure 3.3. The Wagners' Family PBS Self-Check.

Explanations of Categories

Family Vision and Expectations

Shared values and goals: Every family member can describe what values (e.g., trust, kindness) and/or goals (e.g., spending time together, completing tasks) the family embraces.

Clear behavioral expectations: We all can clearly state what behaviors (e.g., communicating openly, helping with tasks) are expected of the members of our family.

Rules regarding misbehavior: We can all identify behaviors that violate the expectations, as well as the likely results or consequences of those behaviors.

Household responsibilities: Each family member can describe their personal responsibilities (e.g., tasks to maintain the household).

Organization of Space and Time

Good household organization: The physical arrangement in our home is conducive to positive behavior (e.g., items are where they are needed, everyone has personal space).

Shared family calendar: We maintain a calendar (e.g., written, electronic) that includes all of the events in which coordination of activities is necessary.

Consistent daily routines: We have predictable family routines (e.g., getting ready, making the transition to school/work, completing self-care and daily living tasks).

Notice of schedule changes: We communicate with one another in advance when we need to change our plans (e.g., canceling or changing events, returning home late).

Time limits on activities: We have established limits on how much time is allowed and when activities (e.g., screen time, guest visits, curfews) may occur.

Teaching and Basic Discipline

Explaining and modeling: We clearly describe our expectations, showing other family members how we would like them to behave or perform tasks through our behavior.

Praise for positive behavior: We acknowledge and say positive things to one another when family members pitch in, are kind to us, or accomplish something important.

Privileges linked to behavior: Family members are more likely to gain access to special activities, treats, allowance, or other preferred things when behaving in accordance with expectations.

Pre-planned consequences: Everyone can predict what consequences are likely to follow a particular behavior (e.g., losing privileges for violating household rules).

Respectful discipline methods: We focus on logical and natural consequences (i.e., those tied to the behavior, such as replacing items that are broken) instead of more punitive measures.

Figure 3.4. Explanations of each category on the Family PBS Self-Check.

Explanations of Categories *(continued)*

Supporting Family Life
Open, clear communication: We consistently tell each other what we are thinking and what we need so that lines of communication remain open.
General respect and kindness: We treat each other as we would want to be treated, demonstrating empathy, thoughtfulness, and overall respect for one another's needs.
Effective problem resolution: When problems or conflicts occur, we work together to achieve solutions that work for everyone.
Strong, loving relationships: We demonstrate affection for one another and are confident in the love we feel for one another.
Ability to manage stress: We have positive, productive ways of managing stress (e.g., taking breaks, mindfulness, exercise), avoiding taking it out on ourselves or others.
Support of family and friends: We have extended family and friends we can rely on for support and assistance when needed.
Full community participation: We are able to participate in the full range of community activities that are important for our family.

■ ACTIVITY ■ Family PBS Self-Check

Family name: _____

Member(s) responding: _____

Date: _____

Please rate the degree that each of the following is in place by checking the appropriate column.

Family Vision and Expectations	Not at all	Somewhat	Very much
Shared values and goals			
Clear behavioral expectations			
Rules regarding misbehavior			
Household responsibilities			
Organization of Space and Time	Not at all	Somewhat	Very much
Good household organization			
Shared family calendar			

(continued)

Family PBS Self-Check (*continued*)

Consistent daily routines			
Notice of schedule changes			
Time limits on activities			
Teaching and Basic Discipline	**Not at all**	**Somewhat**	**Very much**
Explaining and modeling			
Praise for positive behavior			
Privileges linked to behavior			
Pre-planned consequences			
Respectful discipline methods			
Supporting Family Life	**Not at all**	**Somewhat**	**Very much**
Open, clear communication			
General respect and kindness			
Effective problem resolution			
Strong, loving relationships			
Ability to manage stress			
Support of family and friends			
Full community participation			

As with everything in this book, we encourage you to complete this as a family. Once you have completed the assessment, you should look over it together. It is likely that you may have different perspectives on what you are currently doing—that is okay. Initiating the discussion is always helpful. Keep in mind that this tool is simply to assess what is going on. It should not be used to confront or blame one another. The upcoming chapters help you address challenges you might be facing in a collaborative way. If your children are very young or you have family members with disabilities, then they may not be able to fully participate in this process, but you could ask them questions such as, "What expectations do we have in this family?" or "Do you feel like we listen to you?" As you review your assessments, be sure to note areas in which you feel you are particularly strong and celebrate those! Then prioritize areas of concern together, noting that this tool is aligned with the chapters in this book.

SUMMARY: HOW DO WE GET
STARTED WITH POSITIVE BEHAVIOR SUPPORT?

This book provides tools for assessing current family functioning and use of PBS practices. Tools for assessing current functioning and behavior include the Weekly Family Behavior Rating Tool and Family Interaction Journal. Use these tools to identify how your family is doing and possible patterns that may be affecting behavior.

Although PBS is an individualized approach, there are certain elements of PBS that contribute to family functioning, including family vision and expectations, organization of space and time, teaching and basic discipline, and broader supports to enhance family life. Assessing these features at the outset of the process provides a starting point for planning.

BEFORE MOVING ON

- Have you completed the Weekly Family Behavior Rating Tool and Family Interaction Journal with your family?

- What did you learn about current family behavior and interactions?

- Have you completed the Family PBS Self-Check with your family?

- What did you identify as your strengths and areas of difficulty?

- On what areas would you like to focus going forward?

4 | Creating Your Family Vision and Expectations

Positive, healthy, and productive families know who they are, what they want, and what is expected of all family members. Instead of operating on assumptions or whims, they regularly clarify, update, and restate their expectations and limits. This chapter focuses on these topics. We discuss how to create an overall vision for your family and how to use that vision to develop concrete expectations for family members.

ESTABLISHING A FAMILY VISION

This portion of the chapter guides your family to review your collective vision regarding how you want your family to function. You should focus on goals and aspirations that would most affect your family quality of life—self-advocacy, relationships, productivity, health, and inclusion. As part of this process, you will develop a mission statement that clarifies your family's values, goals, and practices.

Family cohesiveness depends on shared beliefs, values, and goals. Conflict and communication breakdowns can occur when family members disagree about these foundations. That is not to say that family members will all share the same perspectives (they won't), but it is critical to find agreement on certain core values that define your family.

We encourage families to articulate their vision of success, much like effective businesses create mission, vision, and value statements for their organizations. These statements essentially say who you are, what you believe, and how you want to function together. Creating a vision statement

DOWNLOADABLE RESOURCES

You may find the following resource from the *Helping Your Family Thrive* workbook helpful as you read this chapter and complete the activities:

- Family PBS Plan (Family Vision, Family Expectations, and Family Rules sections)

Visit the Brookes Download Hub to obtain this resource for Chapter 4.

may not be as easy as it sounds. It may require you to explore your personal and collective values, share your perspectives on different issues, and build agreements with some degree of negotiation and compromise. A guiding question for this discussion could be, "What comes to mind when you imagine the best possible family?" You might follow that initial question with some of the following:

- What do you do as a family?

- How do you communicate?

- What do you achieve together?

- How do you all like to be treated?

- What roadblocks do you avoid?

- How do you resolve problems?

Exploring your values can be helpful as you are trying to reach a consensus on your family vision. This may involve reflecting on how your own upbringing, culture, or family history have affected your view of family and deciding what aspects of your background you may want to embrace, change, or avoid. One helpful exercise is to circle or rank order the following values individually and then compare them. If important values are missing, then you may add them.

■ ACTIVITY ■ Exploring Our Values

Use the chart to identify the values that are most important to you as a family. Fill in the blank squares with other values that are important to members of your family.

Respect	Kindness	Empathy	Generosity	Honesty
Cooperation	Equality	Achievement	Responsibility	Openness
Integrity	Compassion	Curiosity	Gentility	Creativity
Productivity	Inclusion	Civic duty	Courage	Perseverance
Patience	Enjoyment	Togetherness	Supportiveness	Faith
Forgiveness	Humility	Excellence	Assertiveness	Accountability
Helpfulness	Fairness	Independence	Community	Spirituality

Once you have identified your core values and come to some degree of consensus on your responses to the previous questions, you will summarize your core beliefs into a single statement that describes your family or the family you want to be. This can help to make sure everyone in the family is on the same page. For example, you might say something such as,

"Everyone is working together and getting their needs met to have high-quality family time."

"In the Jones family, we treat each other kindly and take responsibility for our actions."

"All family members feel love, respect, and hope for the future—even during difficult times."

Consider using a process like the Wagners used to select and discuss core values with your family and create a shared vision statement.

The Wagner Family: Creating a Family Vision

The Wagners held a family meeting over pizza dinner and reviewed the list of values shown in a previous figure, considering what they felt each value meant. They talked about which values they thought were similar or overlapped and why. The Wagners always had fun chatting about top 10 lists, so they decided they would choose 10 family values. Each member (except Tristan) chose or created their top 10 list individually. The family did agree they wanted to use simple terms that would be easy to describe or show Tristan as he was growing up. They used the chart and each put a checkmark by their top 10, writing in other values that they felt were important but not on the list. The family members all chose kindness, honesty, and helpfulness. The rest of the values were discussed to see where words may be overlapping in how the family members viewed them. For example, as they discussed courage and perseverance, the family members decided that perseverance for them meant trying new things as well as trying their best, so they chose perseverance. They discussed accountability versus responsibility. Sara and Josef realized that they didn't want to have to hold each member accountable, given their strict family histories, but they felt better about each member learning to take responsibility for their own assignments and actions. The Wagner family's top 10 values were kindness, honesty, responsibility, curiosity, forgiveness, helpfulness, perseverance, community, family first, and fun. The Wagners then let each member craft a sentence for the vision. They put all five visions on a piece of paper, and then they discussed how to combine their individual vision statements into one. Here is what they came up with for their family vision:

The Wagners put family first, and we are responsible, kind, and honest to each other and within our community.

Note that the vision statement is in the present tense, even though you may feel you may need to work to achieve it. Create a vision with your family. You may also wish to write it down here and/or record it in the Family Vision section of your Family Plan.

■ ACTIVITY ■   Vision Statement

Our vision for our family is:

_____

_____

_____

_____

_____

DEVELOPING BEHAVIORAL EXPECTATIONS, RESPONSIBILITIES, AND RULES

Once you have clarified your core family values and goals, you take this process a step further to clarify your expectations for behavior in your household. Parents often assume family members should simply know what to do and what not to do. Usually, that is not the case. Many, if not most, family conflicts arise out of miscommunication about expectations. The guiding questions to be answered in this part of the chapter are the following:

- "What does everyone in this family need to do to realize our vision of success?"

- "What behaviors of family members are likely to interfere with that vision?"

Answering these questions involves developing expectations, responsibilities, and rules for family members.

Expectations

Expectations are statements about what everyone in the household needs to say or do; specifically, how each member should behave to achieve the goals outlined in your vision of success. You need to be as straightforward as possible when setting expectations. This means avoiding vague labels for behavior such as "being nice" or assumptions about intentions such as saying someone is "irresponsible or mean." The following paragraphs list examples of specifics instead of these generalizations. It is best to only have a handful of expectations for behavior, maybe between three and five, so family members can remember them. If you generate a lengthy list of expectations, then look closely at your priorities and see whether your expectations overlap and could be consolidated. As you work with other family members to determine what is most important, it may become apparent what expectations will contribute most to your overall family happiness and productivity.

Expectations should be positively stated, saying what you want members to do, rather than what you want them to stop (e.g., speak respectfully vs. no swearing). Expectations will necessarily be different for families with young children than those with adolescents or young adults. For example, families with young children might have these rules: 1) use gentle hands, 2) speak politely, and 3) pick up your toys. Yet, families with older children might adopt these: 1) keep your belongings organized, 2) complete your chores and homework, and 3) communicate your concerns openly. It is best to write down your behavioral expectations and make them available to all members. They might be tacked on the refrigerator or in a decorative frame (e.g., "In this family, we . . ."). If you have young children or family members with developmental disabilities, then it can be helpful to add pictures to make the expectations understandable for everyone.

When possible, it is beneficial to evaluate the alignment of your family expectations with expectations of other settings in which family members participate. Schools, child care settings, work, recreational programs, and other households your family members regularly visit may have their own expectations for behavior (e.g., asking permission, taking turns, fixing or replacing items that are broken). Many schools use PBS to teach expected behavior to their students and often have an acronym containing three to five positively stated behaviors (see the PAWS example in Chapter 10). These can be a good place to start and can then be adapted to fit your family context. Having the same or similar expectations can reduce the stress family members may experience when expectations are quite different while building greater consistency and continuity across settings. If expectations are different, then you have three choices to consider: 1) see if agreement can be reached or can be kept as close as possible to other settings to create more consistency across settings, 2) teach children to deal with the discrepancies in expectations (e.g., describe and model the differences between expected behaviors across settings), or 3) consider no longer participating in settings where expectations significantly contradict your values (e.g., set limits on time spent at friends' houses where expectations or values are misaligned with your family and/or cause discomfort for any family member, opt out of invitations to spaces that may be overwhelming or unenjoyable for any family member).

Although your household's overall expectations should be consistent, the different roles and responsibilities of the family members require some flexibility. We cannot expect the same behavior from toddlers and teenagers. Parents have more demands and maturity and, therefore, more say in how the household functions. As a parent, you need to have some control in setting the priorities and limits for the rest of the family, especially when health and safety concerns dictate the need to step in. As discussed in Chapter 6, you should tie your expectations to consequences—to reward and correct behavior in order to improve family members' motivation to meet the expectations.

Wagner Family: Defining Expectations

The Wagners continued their efforts to build a clear understanding of how they wanted their family to behave in order to have their best possible lives. They defined five expectations to help guide their family members, and they discussed some of the behaviors that described each expectation. Here is what they came up with.

In the Wagner family, we . . .

1. *Make family time a priority.* Each member, including Sara and Josef, blocks out time for our weekly family meetings and calendar planning time. We honor our commitment to weekly game times. If there is a scheduling conflict, then we discuss it with Mom or Dad in advance or during the weekly family meeting. Before making other plans, we make sure they have been agreed on and communicated to all family members.

2. *Show respect for one another.* We use kind words. We don't swear. We use gentle touches with each other. We don't give others the silent treatment. Instead, we find time to talk about our feelings or concerns. We share our outside interests and activities with each other during family dinners and around the television and during game time. We apologize when we are wrong or have made poor choices.

3. *Demonstrate personal responsibility.* We choose chores that need to be done weekly at the family meeting, and we do them without complaint or constant reminder by Mom and Dad. We review/do our homework the day assigned and ask for help from a sibling or a parent if we don't understand what needs to be done or we need help to complete or schedule the completion. Sara and Josef include their work schedules on the weekly calendar. We don't use others' belongings without express permission.

4. *Take care of our belongings.* We use items for their intended purpose. We don't throw or damage things. We keep our electronics charged and keep the charging cords in the charging drawer for all to use. We put our dirty clothes in our bins in our rooms. The floor is not a place to store clothes, toys, shoes, and so forth—hangers, closets, cubbies, and bins will be labeled and used.

5. *Communicate honestly and in a timely manner.* We ask for help with homework, transportation to events, schedule changes, supplies for homework, and so forth as soon as we are aware of the need. We keep a list of any concerns we want to discuss during our family meetings on the fridge next to the calendar. Any family member may request a meeting at any time. If it can't be arranged right away, then a time will be planned in the next 24 hours. We take interpersonal problems to the person we have an issue with first and try to solve it on our own before we bring in Dad or Mom or other family members.

Complete the following activity to develop family expectations, or, if you prefer, complete the Family Expectations section of the Family Plan document available with the downloadable resources for this book.

■ ACTIVITY ■ Our Family Expectations

Develop no more than seven positively stated expectations with your family.
For each expectation, describe exactly what family members should say or do
(behavior).

1. Expectation:

    _____

    _____

    Desired behavior:

    _____

    _____

    _____

    _____

2. Expectation:

    _____

    _____

    Desired behavior:

    _____

    _____

    _____

    _____

3. Expectation:

    _____

    _____

    Desired behavior:

    _____

    _____

    _____

    _____

4. Expectation:

    _____

    _____

Desired behavior:

_____

_____

_____

_____

5.　Expectation:

_____

_____

Desired behavior:

_____

_____

_____

_____

6.　Expectation:

_____

_____

Desired behavior:

_____

_____

_____

_____

7.　Expectation:

_____

_____

Desired behavior:

_____

_____

_____

_____

Responsibilities

All families have chores they must complete to keep their households running smoothly. Stress and resentment can occur when one or two family members have the responsibility for the vast majority or even all the tasks. Sharing responsibility for chores can enhance family unity and teach children a work ethic that will carry over into adulthood. Yet, a lack of clarity about who should do what and when can lead to conflict.

For these reasons, we encourage you to divvy up your family chores based on each family member's capabilities and preferences. To initiate this planning process, you should determine what exactly needs to be done daily, weekly, monthly, or even on a more extended basis (e.g., including seasonal chores). Examples of everyday family chores include preparing meals, paying bills, feeding and walking pets, collecting and taking out the trash, stacking and emptying the dishwasher, mowing the lawn, bringing in the mail, washing the car, and a variety of other cleaning and maintenance tasks.

Once you have developed a complete list, you can work together to determine what each task entails (what exactly needs to be done to be thorough), who is the best person to complete it, and when it needs to be accomplished. Young children or family members with disabilities may need to do simpler chores such as taking dishes to the sink or putting toys/belongings away. As children get older, they can take on more complex tasks. If family members prefer certain chores, have skills that match what is required, or are only available during certain times of the day due to work, school, or community activities, then these issues should be a factor.

If your family has weekly or monthly chores that need to be completed, another helpful strategy is to develop a list of tasks that need to be accomplished by a particular time. Instead of assigning the chores, family members can work through the list, choosing what they want to do. Anytime you can provide some choice and control, you will find that family members are more cooperative. If needed, develop a chore list for your family that includes all tasks that need to be accomplished each day/week, who is responsible, and when the chore needs to be done.

The Wagners created a chore chart because they had identified Household Responsibilities as an area in which they wanted to improve. The process they followed for identifying and assigning chores is discussed in detail in Chapter 5.

Rules

Rules are the extension and clarification of expectations. Rules are contingency statements that specify what behavior is expected in certain circumstances and will lead to predetermined consequences. Rules help family members predict, "If you do (behavior), then (consequences) will happen." Rules are used to maintain order and safety. They provide limits on activities (e.g., use of electronics, curfews) as well as specify what behaviors would align with and violate expectations. Rules provide clear parameters or boundaries.

Rules should be clear and concise. They should specify what actions are allowable as well as those that are not. Rules must be tied to consequences to be consistently followed and effective (see Chapter 6). Examples of rules might include the following:

- Once your homework and chores are done, you may use your phone or play video games until dinner or bedtime.

- If you damage or misplace your belongings, then you will be responsible for replacing them.

- You must eat your entire dinner if you want dessert or snacks following the meal.

- If you want to hang out with your friends, then you must communicate who (you will be with), what (you will be doing), where (you will be), and when (you will return).

- Avoid talking to strangers because there are people who may hurt you.

In contrast to expectations, rules are often situation specific. You might have rules for when guests come to the house or when you are a house guest. You might have specific rules for places you go in the community (e.g., stores, restaurants, parks). When rules need to change, it is vital to explain those changes in advance, providing a rationale for why the expected behavior needs to be different. For example, you might say, "We will probably be waiting for a while in the doctor's office. If you are bored and need something to do—and remain quiet—you may play video games until we get called back." Another example when traveling might be, "We don't know our way around this area. Therefore, I need you to stay right next to me to stay safe." Parents, as well as children, should abide by the rules whenever possible.

Simply explaining rules may not always be sufficient. Children (and sometimes parents) may test limits. In this case, it is beneficial to put rules in writing. You can record your rules by drafting a behavioral contract in which all parties clarify their responsibilities and sign that they are in agreement with the rules. Parents and older siblings should take the responsibility to teach younger children expectations and rules. Teaching expectations may include modeling expected behavior, explaining why you are choosing to behave in a particular way, and acknowledging mistakes. For example, you might say, "I left this room a mess. I need to clean it up before I head off to bed" or "I came home late without calling. I bet you were worried. I need to be more responsible." Providing praise for successes is also essential for teaching expectations. How to provide recognition effectively is addressed in Chapter 6.

Like expectations, rules will change over time as children mature and new situations arise. Children may need more freedom and responsibility as they get older. If they are testing limits or engaging in unsafe behavior, then it may be necessary to tighten the reins and increase supervision. You may need to reevaluate rules more often and negotiate changes. It is okay to change rules—and even break them from time to time. The key is to be proactive and collaborative in decision making.

Wagner Family: Establishing Rules

Because the Wagner family identified their top challenge areas as Household Responsibilities, Shared Family Calendar, and Pre-planned Consequences, they decided to first clarify and write down rules for those areas:

1. If you complete your weekly chores on time and without reminders, then you may use your electronics when chores are completed.

2. You must complete your chores correctly and on time to get rewards or privileges. Therefore, if you need assistance or clarification, then you must ask right away (not knowing how is not an excuse to skip a chore, and we don't know you need help if you don't ask).

3. If your plans change from what is listed on the Shared Family Calendar, then text all family members and other caregivers (e.g., sister-in-law, grandparents). Failure to do so will likely result in a loss of transportation, tardiness, or an inability to attend the event.

4. If you share all upcoming school deadlines, events, or transportation support needs at the weekly family meetings, then you will be supported. If not, then you will have to arrange for your own transportation, needed supplies, and so forth, and you may miss the deadline or event.

5. All family members' electronics will go into the electronics drawer on silent for dinner and at bedtime. Exceptions can be made during times of an emergency if they are preapproved. For example, if Grandma is having a health issue and she or another family member may need to reach us right away, Josef can have his phone on vibrate at the dinner table.

You can use the space below to create If/First–Then statements defining behaviors and consequences for your family and/or record them in the Family Rules section of your Family Plan.

■ ACTIVITY ■ Our Family Rules

As a family, identify the rules (If/First-Then statements) that are needed for your family. Limit them to no more than seven if possible. Include any limits that are important to maintain your family's expectations.

1. If:

   _____

   _____

   Then:

   _____

   _____

   _____

2. If:

    _____

    _____

    Then:

    _____

    _____

    _____

3. If:

    _____

    _____

    Then:

    _____

    _____

    _____

4. If:

    _____

    _____

    Then:

    _____

    _____

    _____

5. If:

    _____

    _____

    Then:

    _____

    _____

    _____

6. If:

    _____

    _____

Then:

_____

_____

_____

7. If:

_____

_____

Then:

_____

_____

_____

SUMMARY: WHAT IS OUR FAMILY LIKE AT OUR BEST?

A family vision integrates your values and goals into a statement of what you want to be as a family. It provides a north star to guide and ground your efforts as a family in this PBS process.

Behavioral expectations are specifically what you want your family members to say or do to achieve your vision as a family. They can include responsibilities for tasks around the house as well as situation-specific rules that clarify consequences that may follow a particular behavior.

BEFORE MOVING ON

- Have you discussed your values and goals, identifying points of consensus?

- What is your family vision, and how might it affect your priorities?

- Have you developed four to seven behavioral expectations for your family?

- Are the behaviors associated with those expectations clear to all members?

- Have you determined who is responsible for what tasks in the family?

- Have you created rules to guide behavior and clarify consequences?

Arranging Your Family Environment to Promote Success

The way in which our physical and social environments are organized can have a significant impact on family interactions, including how space is used and items are placed around the house, as well as scheduling and routines. In this chapter, we help you consider these issues and ways you might reorganize aspects of your family life to promote the best possible behavior.

ATTENDING TO PHYSICAL ENVIRONMENT

Architects, engineers, educators, and other professionals have long understood that the way we organize our space affects our behavior. This is true in family homes as well. It is not unusual for family members to disagree about who put what where, whose belongings are whose, and whose stuff is lying around and in everyone else's way. Those hassles can be minimized by organizing your stuff and surroundings to better meet the needs of all family members.

As we begin this chapter, it is important to acknowledge that people and families differ in the levels of structure they prefer and the degree of disarray or disorder they can tolerate. Therefore, you want to ask yourself if you feel your household organization is working for you and other family members or if it is contributing to negative interactions and family stress. As with all aspects of family life discussed in this book, there is no right and wrong way, just what works for your family. Some areas to consider when assessing your household organization include the ease of supervision and whether the arrangement leads to productive and positive interactions or disruption and conflict.

Providing Both Supervision and Personal Space

Regarding supervision, family members are less likely to get into trouble and more likely to stay safe when they are accountable for their belongings and easily monitored. When children are young, it is best to have their play areas within earshot and range of vision. As children get older, they want more personal space so they can explore their individuality and develop relationships outside of the home. Too much personal space or being left alone for long periods, however, can lead to a lack of accountability. For this reason, it may be necessary to ask family members to share their plans, including with whom they will be spending time, what they will do, where they will be, and when they will return. Another option is to set a schedule to check in when family members are away from home (e.g., texting or calling every 2 hours).

Establishing personal space for all family members is also important. Children and parents may want a level of sovereignty over their bedrooms or other defined areas (e.g., home office, china cabinet). When your family needs to share space (which is typical), you may want to create personal space for each family member and define any off-limit areas. For example, parents may have closets or drawers that are off limits to other family members. Children sharing space could have crates for their favorite items that slip under their beds or specific shelves or caddies for their own hygiene products. When family members share a room but want to organize or decorate their space differently, it may be helpful to provide a divider (or masking tape separating their areas) so that they can do what they want in their own areas. Headphones and reading lights can also reduce quarrels. Establishing these areas of personal space commonly reduces unnecessary disagreements.

Improving Productivity and Reducing Distractions

Productivity is another consideration in arranging your household. Family members may need quiet spaces to complete work. These might be a den or office, the kitchen table, or a desk in a family member's room. These spaces should be stocked with needed materials (e.g., pens, paper, computers). Families also need to complete chores to sustain the household. Having the necessary cleaning, cooking, gardening, and other supplies on hand and within reach is important to get this work done efficiently. Finally, families need to make the transition to and from work, school, sports, child care, and other settings. Having a specific place for keys, shoes, backpacks, purses, and other items that are needed daily can make these transitions smoother. Arranging specific areas of the home (e.g., those for getting ready or storing belongings) can also increase independence among family members and decrease time wasted looking for lost items.

Finally, you want to consider if arrangements or items create unnecessary distractions or challenges. If you want to have uninterrupted conversations during meals, then you want cell phones set aside or set on silent while eating. If you want your family members to be well rested in the mornings, then it may be best not to have televisions and/or electronic devices in the bedrooms or use parental control apps to shut them off automatically at certain times of day. If you want your children to finish homework before playing, then you may not want their study area by a window where they can see their friends playing outside. If you want to walk safely to get a drink from the kitchen at night, then it is always better to have toys and shoes put away before bedtime or just take a water bottle to bed at night. If clutter makes you crazy, then you want to find ways to contain it (e.g., storing out of sight, getting rid of it). A practice that might work for your family is to have children go through their belongings before events in which they are likely to receive gifts and select a half dozen items to give away. As previously mentioned, these decisions are highly personal. If you find that aspects of your household organization are creating problems for you or other family members, then they are worth changing. Before jumping right to solutions, however, we encourage you to spend a little time observing how your family members use and interact in those spaces. It is much easier to change the physical environment to support the desired behavior than change a person's habits to fit the context.

The Wagner Family: Organizing Household Responsibilities

The Wagner family noted in their checklist that Household Responsibilities were an issue for them. They weren't clear about who was supposed to do what and by when. They created a chore chart to address this issue. It included regular chores and blanks to add extra chores that did not have to occur weekly (e.g., going through clothing to remove items that didn't fit or were damaged, special projects such as changing out the contents of their shelves and planters). The family members drew numbers one through five at the weekly family meeting. Each member then chose a chore from the list in the order of their number. They continued selecting until the chores were all assigned. Since Tristan was 3 years old, whoever drew number three had Tristan help with their chores. Sara and Josef each took one chore away from them because it would take the family member longer to do the chore because they had to teach Tristan. If needed, Sara and Josef would guide the family member assigned to work with Tristan generate ideas about how he may be able to help them with their chores.

   In addition, the Wagner family discussed how hard it was for everyone to get where they needed to be with the right stuff each time they were headed out the door. Therefore, they asked Sara's dad, who was handy with wood, to build them a shelving unit with six columns, one for each family member. Each column had a hook for coats, backpacks, or briefcases, as well as two lower shelves for shoes and homework and other sports, theater, work, or event supplies that they needed to have with them the following day.

   The Wagners got another shelving unit for the family room that included eight baskets. Tristan had three baskets to use for toys and books because the family room served as a play area for him. The other family members had a basket with their name on it for anything they wanted to use in the family room, including school supplies. Each member was asked to stash their stuff in their bin when they left the family room to help keep the floor clean.

Consider different rooms or areas of your home. Draw a floor plan if that is helpful. Identify areas where your interactions tend to be positive and those where disagreements or routine disruptions tend to occur (you may use green and red markers on your floor plan or create two lists of spaces). Identify organizational changes that would help your family in each area where challenges occur, and create a plan for putting these in place. Engage the rest of the family in making these changes.

Complete the following activity to develop organizational strategies for your home, or, if you prefer, complete the Household Arrangement section of the Family Plan document available with the downloadable resources for this book.

■ ACTIVITY ■ Household Arrangement

Develop organizational strategies for different areas of your home.

1. Area:

    _____

    Organizational strategies:

    _____
    _____
    _____
    _____

2. Area:

    _____

    Organizational strategies:

    _____
    _____
    _____
    _____

3. Area:

    _____

Organizational strategies:

_____

_____

_____

_____

4. Area:

_____

Organizational strategies:

_____

_____

_____

_____

5. Area:

_____

Organizational strategies:

_____

_____

_____

_____

ORGANIZING FAMILY TIME

Families can be very busy, with members scrambling to get things done, participating in different activities, and heading in multiple directions. This can create stress, especially when life feels unpredictable, unbalanced, or overwhelming. Therefore, how we organize our time can significantly contribute to the quality of family interactions. Three recommendations for effectively organizing family time are to maintain a family calendar, structure daily routines thoughtfully (and modify any routines that are not working well), and set time lines and limits for certain activities.

Maintaining a Family Calendar

It is beneficial to have a family calendar that integrates all the important details of your family life. Your calendar may be electronic (e.g., a shared Google, iCloud, Outlook, or Yahoo calendar) or written (e.g., a dry erase board on the refrigerator, shared paper calendar—perhaps with different sections or colored writing for each family member). It is important to discuss schedules regularly, regardless of the calendar planning method used (e.g., planning schedules for the upcoming week together every Sunday). The goal is to find a calendar strategy that works for you and your family and fits within your existing systems as much as possible. Calendars may be organized weekly, monthly, or even annually to capture major events.

Your entries on the calendar should include who will be doing what, where, when, for how long, and with whom. If transportation or specific child care arrangements are needed for an activity, then that should be determined as well. Most calendar apps have fields that allow you to enter all the previous information and more when creating a new event, enabling you to capture relevant details, as well as schedule recurring events (i.e., those that repeat on a daily, weekly, or monthly basis) and program alerts of upcoming activities. Including all the critical information about family members' activities and events can help prevent misunderstandings and unnecessary distress. The busier your family is, the more complex your calendar needs to be to keep everything organized.

Calendars should include what we have to do and what we want to do. *Have to* activities include work, school, meals, chores, and hygiene. *Want to* activities include family dinners, movie or game nights, holiday gatherings, sports/exercise, or special outings. Adding *want to* activities to your routine makes enjoyable, family-strengthening events a priority and scheduling less of a chore. If things come up and you need to make changes to your schedule, then you should communicate those changes with your family, noting them on the calendar to make sure everyone in the family is aware. When adding something to your calendar, you may want to consider if something else needs to be moved or changed so that your schedule stays balanced and manageable.

Sometimes arranging events for the whole family can feel like a balancing act: one person needs to do (activity) while others need to be at (place). Negotiating and considering alternative options for arranging activities or supports may be necessary. As a family, you need to determine your priorities based on your values, vision, and expectations, scheduling the most important events first or adjusting your plans. For example, attending a service for a family member who has recently passed away, making sure that your teenager can attend their prom, or attending a meeting regarding a problem that is occurring at school may quickly rise to the top. The schedule should meet everyone's needs, but some things might have to be rearranged or rescheduled as needs arise. Advanced and collaborative planning reduces many conflicts.

The Wagner Family: Family Calendar

The Wagners purchased a set of colored highlighters, and each family member chose a unique color for their scheduled events. They also selected a family color for events in which all members participated. They used a free, printable monthly calendar pulled from the Internet. As new events and work schedules were identified, each member added their new events and timing in pencil and then highlighted the event in their color. The Wagner family calendar is shown in Figure 5.1. Each week after their Saturday dinner, they

Color Key	Month: October						
Sara	Sunday	Monday	Tuesday	Wednesday	Thursday	Friday	Saturday
Josef					**1** Theater 4–6, Parent–teacher conference 5–7	**2** Dr. appointment. 11:00, Band 6:00	**3** Band practice 10–1, Family dinner 5:00
Thom	**4** Bike ride 11:00, Games 4:00	**5** Work 7–7, Soccer 4:00	**6** Work 7–7, Tutor 4:00	**7** Work 7–7, Band 4:00	**8** Theater 4–6, Speech 4:00	**9** Football 6:00, Play date 1:00	**10** Soccer game 2:00, Band competition 11–3, Family dinner 5:00
Shannon	**11** Work 7–7, Games 4:00	**12** Work 7–7, Soccer 4:00	**13** Work 7–7, Tutor 4:00	**14** Work 7–7, Band 4:00	**15** Speech 4:00, New York trip	**16** Band 6:00	**17** YMCA 11:00, Band practice 10–1
Julia	**18** Bike ride 11:00, Family dinner 5:00	**19** Work 7–7, Soccer 4:00 with Mom	**20** Work 7–7, Tutor 4:00	**21** Work 7–7, Meeting 6:00	**22** Theater 4–6, Speech 4:00	**23** Play date 1:00	**24** Movies 8:00
Tristan	**25** YMCA 11:00, Family dinner 5:00 with Mom	**26** Work 7–7, Soccer 4:00	**27** Work 7–7, Tutor 4:00	**28** Work 7–7	**29** Theater 4–6, Speech 4:00	**30**	**31** Trick or treat party 5–11
All							

Notes:
Josef works 8–6 M–F
Tristan is in child care 7:30–6:30 M–W

Figure 5.1. The Wagners' family calendar.

went over the calendar and reviewed the upcoming 2 weeks to see what had been added/updated since the last week. They planned any materials, transportation, and scheduling adjustments that were needed (e.g., shifting dinner plans).

If you already have a family calendar, then consider whether it includes the necessary details and is balanced in terms of everyone's needs and includes both *have to* and *want to* activities. If you do not currently have a family calendar (one that includes all overlapping family activities), then work with your family to research options or develop one using one of the formats suggested here that works for your family. (A blank form to get you started is included in your Family Plan.)

Thoughtfully Structuring Daily Routines

In addition to a shared weekly or monthly calendar, it is beneficial to assess how your daily routines are working for your family. Routines are activity sequences that occur at regular times. They are how we organize our time in the moment. You probably have routines for getting ready in the morning; meals; transitions to and from work, school, and other places; chores; homework; and bedtime. When you find you are experiencing hassles during a particular routine, that is your signal to redefine expectations or steps to complete that routine. For example, when sharing a bathroom, your family members may argue about who gets to do what when. If so, you may want to sort out the order of who has access to the bathroom and establish time limits. Whoever needs to leave the house first might have priority, but they also need to respect the time lines of other family members. When work tasks or homework needs to be completed, you may want to set aside particular periods during the day and clarify how other family members will keep themselves busy until it is done.

Finding ways to share responsibility is also important. For example, when trying to get meals on the table for a busy family, you may want to divvy up tasks, deciding who will set the table, prepare different parts of the meal, and clean up afterward. When trying to get out of the door in the morning, you can make sure each family member is clear on what they need to do to pitch in so no one runs late. For example, individual family members might be responsible for walking the dog, putting away breakfast items, turning off the lights, and checking that doors are locked, whereas everyone is expected to collect their own belongings (which are hopefully in a designated place, as previously discussed).

The Wagner Family: Structuring Routines for Meals and Mornings

After Sara's realization that the weekly family dinner was falling apart, she and Josef thought about what needed to change so they could get back to having at least one enjoyable meal per week together. Given that their work schedules varied week to week, they agreed they would schedule a family dinner on a Friday, Saturday, or Sunday at 5 p.m. every week. On those days, Thom, Shannon, or Julia could make plans with friends no earlier than 7:30 p.m. Sara loved cooking, so she wanted to know she could plan and prepare at least one nice meal per week without needing to be multitasking. Josef agreed that he would use the dinner prep time as a dedicated playtime with Tristan, to keep him busy and make sure he was getting one-to-one time. Josef agreed that he would not work or check emails during the weekly meal day. They set up the rule that all electronics had to be in the drawer during all mealtimes.

Josef and Sara talked to the kids about tasks for which they wanted help for the weekly family dinner, asking what each person wanted to do. Thom picked setting the table before dinner and cleaning the table. Shannon picked putting dishes in the dishwasher. Julia loved helping Mom cook, so she chose that as well as being responsible for napkins on the table. Josef agreed to wipe down the table and counters.

Given their busy schedules, the Wagners decided to combine family dinners with meetings. After dinner and clean up, everyone got their individual calendars for the family meeting. They went through the upcoming 2 weeks and made any needed updates and transportation plans. They also talked about what was going well and any challenges they were experiencing, brainstorming solutions. When the family meetings were over, anyone who did not have plans would hang around for movie night.

Getting everyone out the door in a timely, stress-free manner during the work/school week was another challenge for the Wagners, so they created a routine for their mornings. The first step was that each individual took responsibility for preparing their own lunch for the following day. Leftovers, sandwich supplies, and fruit choices were first come, first serve unless a member got something special from a friend or for a birthday, holiday, and so forth that they didn't have to share. Because the Wagners were a large family, they put a small refrigerator by the back door for all lunches so they didn't take up space in the kitchen fridge.

Before bed, each member was responsible for putting their needed school work and extracurricular supplies in their shelving space by the back door so that family members weren't scrambling for things in the mornings. Sara or Josef took care of Tristan's lunch and supplies based on who was dropping him off at preschool or another family member's house the next morning. If Sara didn't work the next day, then she did all of the Tristan planning and care.

Thom and Shannon had their own alarm clocks to wake them. Because Julia was sensitive to loud sounds, her alarm clock had a music player, and she got up to her favorite Disney or theater music. She had to let Sara or Josef know she was up so she wasn't tempted to lie in bed and listen causing her to run late. Julia had her morning routine mapped out in a First-Then Visual Scheduler on her iPad so she didn't forget what she needed to do. Each task (e.g., using the bathroom, saying good morning to her parents, washing her face) had a picture and music to go with it, and she checked them off as she completed each one.

The kids' bathroom was used in order of who needed to leave for school first: Thom for high school, Julia for elementary, and Shannon for middle school. Each of the kids got 20 minutes in the bathroom and had to do the rest of their preparations in their bedrooms. Tristan used the master bathroom, with Sara or Josef helping him based on which parent was dropping him off that morning.

For breakfast, the family set up a shelf in the pantry with cereal, granola bars, instant oatmeal, dried fruit, and bread to make toast. There was a fruit drawer in the fridge, and the expectation was that each family member would make their own breakfast that included one pantry item and some fruit. Josef prepared the coffee pot the night before, and Thom or the first adult awake turned it on when they got up. He also filled the hot water pot so it was easy to prepare oatmeal. Sara and Josef shared responsibility for making Tristan's breakfast. The Wagners bought a toaster oven, reducing fighting over whose toast got to go in first. After breakfast, everyone was expected to put their own rinsed dishes in the dishwasher. If the dishwasher had clean dishes in it, then all rinsed dishes got stacked in the sink. Plates and bowls were located so that even Julia could reach them to make her own breakfast.

The final part of the Wagner routine was that right before they left the house, they would say good-bye, hug, or high-five whoever else was in the kitchen so that at least one person knew they were leaving and the day started on a good note. Thom drove to school, and Shannon and Julia both walked to the bus stop with friends.

Structuring routines involves identifying who will do what, when, and in what order. Identify one or more routines that are challenging for your family. Working together, determine how you could modify the routines to make them go smoother for your family. These may include

- Restructuring the layout of the physical setting and reorganizing the materials

- Adjusting the sequence in which tasks or activities occur and setting new expectations

- Modifying your interactions within the routine (e.g., using reminders, providing frequent and consistent feedback)

- Reassigning responsibilities of family members based on their individual abilities and preferences

- Providing more instruction to complete tasks and/or establishing incentives (see Chapter 6).

Complete the following activity to develop strategies for modifying routines in your home, or, if you prefer, complete the Routine Planning section of the Family Plan document available with the downloadable resources for this book.

◼ ACTIVITY ◼ Routine Planning

List any challenging routines in your household and ideas for how your family could modify them.

1. Routine:

   _____

   Changes to organization, sequence, or interactions:

   _____
   _____
   _____
   _____

2. Routine:

   _____

   Changes to organization, sequence, or interactions:

   _____
   _____
   _____
   _____

3. Routine:

   _____

   Changes to organization, sequence, or interactions:

   _____
   _____
   _____
   _____

Setting Time Lines and Limits

A final area we consider regarding time is the need for some type of parameters, time lines, or limits on activities. For example, given your expectations and vision for your family, you may want to minimize screen time or require that an amount of time each day be devoted to other activities such as exercise, reading, worship, and projects. You may also want to welcome visitors to your home only during certain hours of the day/days of the week and/or set aside particular times to spend just with family. You may require family members to check in periodically when away from the house. Such a time line improves accountability.

Time lines also include deadlines. You likely have established curfews (e.g., you must be in the house by dark; 11:00 p.m. on weekdays, 1:00 a.m. on weekends), which get later and more flexible as children age. Time lines can include when particular chores need to be completed. For example, your family might agree that chores are completed by noon on Saturday or before leaving the house to hang out with friends. You may find that time lines are even necessary for seemingly little issues such as how long family members are allowed to let the shower run, thereby leaving hot water for others. Putting a timer in the bathroom to signal a 10-minute limit could help.

Establishing time lines is important for adults as well as children. If your family is going to be cohesive and comfortable, then you may not want everyone coming and going at all hours or busying themselves with work or video games that interfere with family interactions. As parents, we have a special responsibility to model self-restraint and how to balance our time sensibly. If we have established consequences for exceeding time lines, then we should be willing to also model acceptance of the consequences (e.g., "I have been on my phone too much today. I'm going to put it away for the evening so I can focus on our family"). Although time lines are important, there will be times when you may want to break your rules, maybe to binge-watch a favorite program on a rainy day. If your family decides to make this exception once in a while, then it is absolutely fine, provided exceptions do not become the norm.

The Wagner Family: Setting Time Lines and Limits

The Wagner family spent part of one family meeting after their calendar review talking about time lines and limits they thought might help the family function better and meet their value of having fun. These included limits on work for the adults, limits on television and other screen time, and curfews.

Josef agreed that his work at home time had pushed into both the family meal and their game or movie times. He made a commitment to block off those planned times as a no-work intrusion time. Sara had been picking up two to four extra shifts at work, and the family agreed that one extra day per month would be the most she would pick up unless the hospital had an emergency. The family didn't necessarily need her additional income because Josef was promoted, and it was cutting into the family time they wanted.

The kids were limited to an hour of screen time beyond schoolwork or e-books per day. All family members were limited to 1 hour of television time per day during the week and 3 hours per day on the weekend. Television time includes watching shows on personal electronics. Per their rules, homework and chores must be done first for all members of the family unless an exception was granted (e.g., a school snow day).

Kids' social activities on school nights that were not required for marching band, soccer, or theater had to be preapproved by Sara or Josef, and a curfew was set at that time. Thom had to be home on the weekends by 11:30 p.m. and Shannon by 10:30 p.m., unless they had prearranged to stay overnight at a friend's house. Thom had been really pushing back on his 11:30 p.m. curfew with Josef and Sara because his curfew at his Mom's house was 1:00 a.m. on non-school nights, and his band was trying to get more weekend gigs. We will talk about how the family tackled Thom's push back on his curfew later in the book.

Complete the following activity to develop time lines and limits for your family, or add these to the Time Lines and Limits for Activities section of the Family Plan document available with the downloadable resources for this book.

■ ACTIVITY ■ Time Lines and Limits

Working together as a family, determine what time lines and limits are needed in your household.

1. Activity:

    _____

    Time line/limit:

    _____

    _____

    Rationale:

    _____

    _____

    _____

    _____

2. Activity:

    _____

    Time line/limit:

    _____

    _____

    Rationale:

    _____

    _____

    _____

    _____

3. Activity:

    _____

Time line/limit:

_____

_____

Rationale:

_____

_____

_____

_____

SUMMARY: HOW CAN WE BETTER ORGANIZE OUR SPACE AND TIME?

The way in which your household is arranged and organized can affect family behavior. In arranging your physical environment, you may want to consider what level of supervision is available, whether family members have personal space, and how items are organized to maximize productivity or success while minimizing distractions.

Managing family time is a balancing act. Many families find it beneficial to maintain a shared family calendar that includes all activities that affect more than one family member. In addition, it is often helpful to reorganize routines and establish specific time lines for activities.

BEFORE MOVING ON

- Have you identified areas within your home in which organization may be an issue?

- Have you rearranged those areas to improve your family functioning as articulated in your family vision?

- Have you created a shared family calendar and a plan for keeping it current?

- Did you identify any family routines that were challenging? If so, were you able to restructure them to work better for everyone?

- Do you need to establish time lines for certain activities (e.g., curfews, device use)?

6

Teaching Behavioral Expectations

To this point, this book has focused on clarifying expectations and organizing your space and time to support desirable behavior. These steps are certainly helpful but are not enough. You may need to help family members develop new habits to establish new skills or increase how often, how long, or how well behaviors needed to meet your expectations occur. This involves teaching and responding to behavior productively. In this chapter, we begin by discussing how to promote positive behavior through teaching skills family members may not have yet. In the latter sections, we discuss how to respond to behavior in ways that increase positive, expected behaviors and reduce challenging behaviors.

DOWNLOADABLE RESOURCES

You may find the following resource from the *Helping Your Family Thrive* workbook helpful as you read this chapter and complete the activities:

• Family PBS Plan (Teaching Plan and Responding to Behavior sections)

Visit the Brookes Download Hub to obtain this resource for Chapter 6.

PROMOTING POSITIVE BEHAVIOR

A big mistake we can make as parents is to assume that family members know how to do what we are asking but choose not to follow through. Family members may not be motivated to follow rules and participate in routines—that is true (we address this in the next section), but what if they are motivated but do not know exactly what to do or how to do it?

Identifying Skills for Improvement

Before simply resorting to correcting behavior, consider what skills family members may be missing that would help them participate more independently and cooperatively with family expectations. Common skill deficits that may challenge families include:

- Communication (appropriate ways to tell others what they need, want, prefer, or find intolerable)

- Social interaction (skills that allow a person to interact more effectively with other people)

- Organization (skills for managing their own space/belongings and time as well as completing tasks in a timely and effective manner)

- Daily living (skills that allow a person to adapt to the demands of their surroundings and be as independent as possible)

- Problem solving (skills and strategies that enable a person to generate solutions to complex problems)

- Self-management (skills that allow a person to tolerate circumstances and regulate their behavior and emotions)

- Leisure skills (ways to occupy themselves, manage boredom, and experience satisfaction)

This list may be helpful in identifying skills family members may be missing, but it is certainly not exhaustive. Asking yourself, "Does _____ know how to _____?" can be helpful.

Once you know what skills are needed, the first step in teaching them is to define exactly what the behaviors look or sound like. Examples of skills for family members of different ages and abilities are provided in Figure 6.1.

Breaking Complex Skills Into Manageable Parts

Depending on family members' ages and abilities, it may be helpful to break more complex skills down even further into components or steps. For example, the components or steps necessary for a person to engage in a back-and-forth conversation may include the following:

- Wait for the right time and place to talk.

- Get the person's attention with a greeting.

- Ask questions relevant to the person, topic, or context.

- Listen to and acknowledge their answers.

- Respond to questions asked by the other person.

- Wait for pauses in the conversation to talk.

- Share information that is relevant to the conversation.

- Pay attention to the person's tone and body language.

- End the conversation with an appropriate salutation.

Category	Examples of skills
Communication	• Ask for help or 5 more minutes to finish an activity • Express concerns in a respectful and appropriate manner • Set clear limits for acceptable behavior in relationships
Social interaction	• Greet other people when they arrive in the home/setting • Engage in a give-and-take conversation with someone • Express empathy when others are facing difficulty
Organization	• Organize or store belongings in a consistent location • Remain focused and engaged until homework is done • Create "to do" lists or a daily schedule of activities
Daily living	• Bathe, dress, and groom oneself independently • Apply basic first aid to care for a minor injury • Take initiative to complete household maintenance chores (e.g., cooking, laundry, cleaning, lawn work)
Problem solving	• Explain when a toy or appliance is not working properly • Brainstorm solutions to a problem, considering pros and cons • Plan and implement a course of action to tackle a problem
Self-management	• Identify how one's own behavior affects other people • Plan goals and provide own rewards for achievement • Admit to mistakes and take responsibility for actions • Engage in stress reduction practices (e.g., deep breathing)
Leisure skills	• Play independently for periods of time appropriate to age • Identify and set aside time to engage in preferred activities • Participate in recreational activities (e.g., sports, clubs)

Figure 6.1. Examples of skills within seven common skill deficit areas.

Modeling and Role Playing

Once the skills have been defined, you may explain them and model them as necessary. Role playing might help for particularly difficult situations. For example, you might say, "I know you are really angry with your Dad. Let's talk through what you are going to say to sort through this." To model the skill, you would show them exactly what you might say or do. As they say, practice makes perfect. If the family member is willing, then you can have them demonstrate what they will do and provide feedback and suggestions for improvement, possibly practicing multiple times for challenging or novel skills. It may be particularly helpful to remind them of their plan right before they go into the situation. The steps will need to be simplified for family members who are young or have disabilities, and they may require visual reminders. Once the family member has established the skill, you should reduce your guidance and support as quickly as possible, encouraging their independence. It is also important to follow family members' success with new skills by providing immediate, positive social consequences, which is addressed later in the chapter.

Sara Wagner used the approaches previously described to help her children better meet expectations for one kitchen chore. As you read on, think about how Sara identified skills her children lacked; how she taught these skills by explaining, modeling, and breaking them down as needed; and how she helped her children become more independent in using the skills she had taught them.

Wagner Family: Teaching Skills for Household Chores

As the Wagner family considered their routines and responsibilities, it became increasingly apparent that skill deficits were contributing to their difficulties. Sara found herself re-loading and re-running the dishwasher several times a week so it was arranged for proper clearing and maximizing how much could fit. She was getting frustrated, thinking maybe she should just do it herself when a lightbulb went on—she had never shown her kids how the dishes should go in the dishwasher; she had just assumed the kids knew. After the next family dinner, Sara asked Shannon, Thom, and Julia to watch her load the dishwasher so she could show them where the dishes went in the machine and why. They discussed separating the silverware to make unloading it easier, putting spoons up so they don't nest together and forks and knives down to prevent stabbing yourself during the unloading process. She explained that plasticware goes up top to prevent melting and showed them how to lean the bowls so they don't trap a bunch of water. They also discussed which pots and pans are too big to go in the dishwasher and would need to be washed by hand. Shannon and Julia took pictures of the top and bottom racks so they could use the photos as a reminder in the future. They agreed that for the next 2 weeks, Sara would take a quick look before the dishwasher was run and provide any feedback.

Working on New Skills Together

Family members often share overlapping areas of skill deficits due to shared environments, similar personality traits, challenges related to disabilities, lack of exposure to practice opportunities, or other reasons. Developing skills should be a family affair, with children and adults working together to learn or improve. Parents who acknowledge their own challenges may come to recognize and address their own skill deficits and work on skills alongside their children. Sometimes each family member is working on different skills, and other times the areas of skill deficit overlap. Either way, actively working on teaching new skills together as a family provides a wonderful opportunity for modeling and feedback among family members. Although children and adults learn new skills through similar approaches, they often need to apply the same skills differently due to different demands and expectations across environments and developmental stages.

Josef Wagner used his own area of difficulty at work to encourage the development of a new skill for him and his son, Thom. As you read, notice how Josef was able to recognize his own skill deficit and used that awareness to encourage Thom to work on the same skill alongside him. Think about the ways that Josef and Thom used what they learned differently to meet their own needs in their own environments.

The Wagner Family: Learning Skills for Time Management

One of the biggest challenges facing the Wagner family was that they were busy people trying to juggle lots of commitments. In particular, Josef was having difficulty keeping up with the responsibilities of his new position (especially emails), which often kept him from family activities. Thom was staying up later and later to do homework. Josef talked with someone in the human resources department at his workplace and she suggested an online time management course. Josef invited Thom to take the course with him. Through the course, they learned some basic principles: 1) keep a calendar that includes tasks as well as appointments, 2) if you add something, then take something else away, 3) include enjoyable activities on your calendar, and 4) have a consistent routine for planning and reflection. They used these principles to come up with unique strategies.

Josef decided to schedule the last hour of every workday to clean out his email box and plan his priority work for the next day. He realized that he did not have a clear view of the priorities at work or the responsibilities of other members of his team. He spoke with his supervisor and she helped him focus on what was most important and told him which tasks could be delegated to others. Instead of playing catch-up during the weekday evenings, Josef decided that he would work for 2–3 uninterrupted hours on Saturday before the children typically awoke.

Thom purchased an old large tablet for his room that couldn't do much with apps anymore but could display his Google calendar and Google task list with both his personal and school accounts added. Thom entered his band practices and other regular activities. As he made plans with friends or for study groups, he added them. He used the Google task list to document his assigned homework each week and gave each task an assigned date and time to complete it based on his availability. As he completed each homework task, he marked it complete, watching his tasks dwindle as the week went by. Using an old tablet worked well as Thom's visual display because his Google calendar and tasks could easily be updated on his phone while at school or with the band, and the tablet was portable as he moved between his Dad's and Mom's homes every 2 weeks. When Thom finished his daily task list, he used the remaining time to practice and listen to music, binge-watch programs, play video games, or talk or text with friends.

Fostering Independence

Our ultimate goal as parents is for our children to become as independent as possible. That means they are not waiting around for instruction; instead, they take initiative and resolve their own problems. For this reason, we want to emphasize self-management to the greatest extent possible. Rather than telling family members what to do (giving them fish), we want to give them the space and guidance to make their own decisions and regulate their own behavior (learning to fish). To help family members become self-reliant, we need to encourage those self-monitoring and self-management skills and gradually decrease the assistance we provide.

Complete the following Teaching Plan activity to get started on a plan for teaching any skills needed in your family. Or, if you prefer, use the Teaching Plan section of the Family PBS Plan available with the downloadable *Helping Your Family Thrive* workbook. First, identify a skill a family member (or family members, including yourself) need to develop to better adhere to your family expectations and/or routines. Define the skill, listing the steps as needed. Plan how you can explain, model, remind, practice, and provide feedback for the skill. Determine how success in the skill will be defined (e.g., "Tony puts all appointments and tasks in his calendar, checking them off as completed, for an entire week").

■ ACTIVITY ■ Teaching Plan

Skill to be taught:

_____

Definition/steps:

_____

_____

_____

_____

_____

_____

Plan for teaching (explain, model, remind, practice, and/or give feedback):

_____

_____

_____

_____

_____

_____

Plan to gradually reduce guidance:

_____

_____

_____

Criteria for success:

_____

_____

_____

RESPONDING TO BEHAVIOR

Behavior is maintained by the consequences that follow it—what people get or avoid. If what we do (e.g., helping someone) results in positive outcomes (e.g., praise), then we are more likely to behave that way in the future. If our behavior (e.g., complaining, making excuses) allows us to get out of unpleasant situations or arduous tasks, then that consequence may also increase the future rate of occurrence of the behavior. On the flip side, if our behavior results in consequences that are punitive (e.g., losing items or privileges, being scolded), then we are less likely to engage in that behavior going forward.

These concepts of reinforcement (increasing the future likelihood of a behavior through the consequences that follow) and punishment (decreasing the future rate of behavior through the consequences that follow) are important in family life. In this section of the chapter, we address how to increase and maintain desirable behavior and, when necessary, discourage rule breaking through logical and natural consequences.

Encouraging Desired Behavior

Your behavioral expectations and rules specify what you want family members to do and say in your home. To increase the desired behaviors, you want to make sure that they consistently result in positive outcomes for the person. Positive outcomes can come in many forms, including:

- Giving specific praise to the person
- Engaging in preferred activities together
- Giving them tangible rewards
- Reducing or removing demands on them
- Giving them choice and control over a situation
- Linking consequences to behavior

Regardless of the positive outcome, it will be most effective if it is clearly linked to the desired behavior.

Giving Praise   Social praise, or simply acknowledging desirable behavior, is easy to deliver and often has a powerful impact on family members' behavior—even more so when praise has been previously paired with highly preferred activities, events, or items. For example, you might say, "The kitchen looks spotless. Thank you for cleaning all the dishes and wiping down the counters," or "I know how hard it was to ignore your brother's whining, but you did a great job." These responses are very descriptive, stating exactly what the family member did. If you can respond in this way to desirable behavior more often than you correct misbehavior, then you will see adherence to expectations increase.

Doing Preferred Activities Together   Spending time with your family members doing things you both (or all) enjoy can also be highly motivating. You might say something such as, "As soon as we knock out these chores, let's make sandwiches and head to the park." Alternating nonpreferred activities with preferred activities can keep behavior on track. It can be helpful to use first–then language to encourage this alternating of activities (e.g., "First finish your homework, then we can go outside and play." "First eat your vegetables, then you can have dessert"). The second, more desirable, activity then serves as a reinforcer for completing the first.

Giving Tangible Rewards   You can also use tangible rewards, such as preferred items or activities. You might make screen time contingent on following household expectations and/or completing work that needs to be done around the house. It is important to recognize that preferences vary from person to person. You want to make sure that any item or activity provided is motivating to the family member(s) receiving the item. You can identify family members' preferences by asking them or watching how they spend their time; however, you will only know if something is effective if it increases (or maintains) the behavior that it follows. You also need to make sure that the item or activity is only accessible when desired behavior occurs. If access is unlimited or the family member can get the item or privilege on their own, then it will be ineffective as a reward.

Reducing or Removing Demands   As previously mentioned, getting out of unpleasant situations or decreasing the level of demands can actually increase desired behavior. For example, you might say something such as, "You have really been pitching in with the pets lately. How about I walk the dog for you today?" Providing help can also reward desired behavior. You could simply begin assisting with weeding the garden when other family members are working hard or offer to help them research some information for a project they have been working hard to complete. By reducing, delaying, or removing these demands, contingent on desired behavior, you can reward both the behavior itself and positive effort.

Giving Choice and Control   Choice and control can be particularly powerful as well. For example, instead of simply assigning chores, you could create a list and allow each family member to pick what they want to do. Although nobody in the family may like the chores, having the ability to do what they prefer (and avoid less pleasant tasks) is motivating. You may also associate freedom and a diminished need for supervision with behaviors that demonstrate respect and responsibility, especially with more mature family members. For example, because a family member consistently completes tasks and is accountable for their whereabouts, you might say, "I trust you to follow through, so you may set your own daily goals and schedule."

Linking Consequences to Behavior   Positive consequences work best when they are provided right after desired behavior, or are at least clearly linked to it. Most older children and adults can typically tolerate some delay (e.g., waiting for a pizza to be delivered) because they may have a better understanding of time; whereas others, particularly younger children and those with intellectual disabilities, may need more immediate feedback and rewards. If using tangible rewards such as toys or snacks, then you probably want to consider whether you want to use them in the long haul. You can gradually phase them out and shift to natural outcomes such as praise and privileges or retain them only for difficult tasks. Using tokens or points that can be exchanged later for tangible rewards can also be helpful (e.g., putting a sticker on the calendar each day the children "use gentle hands" and then going for ice cream at the end of the week if the goal is achieved). Allowance may eventually be best used only for completing weekly chores.

We want to encourage desired behavior and replace challenging behavior through these positive outcomes. For example, you might praise family members for sharing belongings rather than arguing over them, complimenting rather than teasing, or leaving the room instead of escalating a conflict. If your goal is to compete with consequences a family member gets through undesirable behavior, then the reward for desirable behavior must be stronger (e.g., better, more immediate, larger) than what a family member is currently getting in response to misbehavior (e.g., attention, delaying or reducing the complexity of homework). This is further discussed in the next chapter.

Discouraging Rule Breaking

Sometimes structure and positive outcomes are not enough to produce desired behavior change. For example, one or more family members may engage in behavior that is unsafe, violates the rights of others (e.g., invading their privacy, taking their property), or is highly disruptive to family life. If this is the case, you may need to consider other consequences to reduce these behaviors. These consequences may involve withholding positive outcomes, allowing natural consequences to occur, or planning other consequences for more serious behavior.

Withholding Positive Outcomes   As a first option, we recommend simply withholding rewards and other positive outcomes you would typically provide for desired behavior. Keep in mind the four functions of behavior introduced in Chapter 1—gaining attention; obtaining items or activities; escaping, avoiding, or delaying tasks or situations; and sensory stimulation (see Table 1.1). For example, if a behavior is motivated by attention (e.g., arguing or teasing to get a reaction), then you can strategically ignore it or limit attention as much as possible. If a behavior is maintained by avoiding demands such as chores or homework, then you can teach your child to self-advocate and negotiate while still holding them accountable for completing their tasks. If a behavior is driven by gaining access to items or activities (e.g., nagging for the car keys), then you may prompt them to ask more nicely and delay providing them until the behavior stops. Withholding these outcomes may not be as easy as it sounds. Family members may be accustomed to getting certain reactions or results and may become frustrated when they do not occur. You may need support and perseverance to at least minimize these outcomes for challenging behavior. For a more in-depth discussion of how to handle behavioral challenges, see the companion volume to this book, *Resolving Your Child's Challenging Behavior: A Practical Guide to Parenting With Positive Behavior Support* (Hieneman, Elfner, & Sergay, 2022).

Allowing Natural Consequences to Occur   Some behaviors have their own natural consequences (i.e., they produce unpleasant outcomes). For example, if a family member smashed the video controls when upset at losing a game, then they will not be able to play for a while. If a family member says something insulting to a friend, then they may damage or lose that relationship. In these types of circumstances, allowing consequences to play out or helping your family member make the connection between their behavior and the natural consequences is an effective strategy. It may take multiple learning opportunities, but the family member's behavior is likely to change from these experiences.

Planning Other Consequences You may find it necessary to resort to other planned consequences when infractions are more serious. These often stem from the expectations, rules, and limits discussed in previous chapters, and these are ideally discussed and agreed on as a family before the challenging behavior occurs. Planned consequences may include removing privileges, increasing supervision or decreasing independence, getting restitution for damaged items or relationships, or enlisting specific supports from other family members or from professionals in situations that involve dangerous behaviors. For example, if a family member misses curfew and does not communicate their whereabouts, then you might withhold access to the car or limit their independence (e.g., not being allowed to go out with friends the following weekend). If a family member breaks something that belongs to someone else, then you may require them to fix or replace it or work off the cost by completing extra chores. If a family member hurts someone else, then apologies may not be enough. You might encourage the family member to stay away from them until their behavior improves or require the aggressor to help the person they hurt with their daily chores. If a family member is a danger to themselves or others, then you should seek assistance from trained professionals or legal authorities.

It is important to note that the punishment should fit the crime. Being a couple minutes late for curfew is less serious than showing up the next morning. Your consequences should be logical, natural, and aligned with the seriousness of the behavior in question. It is important that all family members understand the possible consequences of their actions by setting clear expectations from the outset.

Punishment tends to have side effects (e.g., emotional reactions, escalation of behavior) and is situation specific. For this reason, it should be used sparingly, in an even-handed manner, and only in combination with proactive strategies and rewarding desired behavior. You want to avoid becoming coercive—making threats, one-upping the family member, or using consequences that benefit you instead of teaching (e.g., grounding your teen so they must babysit). If you find that you are getting upset when imposing consequences, then you should step away for a few minutes, take some deep breaths, and ask yourself what you might be able to do to prevent or diffuse the situation more effectively or shift your focus back to what you want to achieve in the situation. The clearer the consequences up front, the less likely these types of problems will emerge.

It is important to recognize that not all consequences are within your control. You need to consider what leverage you have. For example, having adult children at home is a challenge many families are facing. They have a right to make their own decisions about their lifestyles, but they do not have the right to take advantage of other family members or disrupt the household (e.g., being late, being loud at night). Whether you make them dinner or pay their automobile insurance may be within your control, but other consequences may not. It is important to never threaten a consequence for which you may not be able to follow through.

The most important leverage is the relationship your family members have with one another. Consequences can be negotiated in a calm and respectful way, and they tend to be more accepted when relationships are strong and there is mutual trust and love. Power struggles are less likely to occur when your emphasis is on encouraging and rewarding desired behavior. Continually investing time and energy into sustaining relationships will reduce the need for punitive and reactive methods (see Chapter 8).

The Wagner Family: Managing Consequences for Chores and Curfews

The Wagners really liked to get chores done promptly and without push-back so they instituted Taco Tuesdays. If everyone's chores were done by Monday evening with no complaining, then the family got to order tacos from their favorite restaurant for dinner. If someone didn't get their chores done by Monday night, then that person had to cook the tacos for the family on Tuesday, and they got kitchen duty that night as well. Sara and Josef were included in the plan. The kids started monitoring each other and Mom and Dad to get their chores done because they preferred the restaurant tacos.

Curfews were important for Thom and Shannon, given their ages. The Wagners put a few things in place to manage the kids' curfews. When either of the kids were out in the evenings and Sara and Josef planned to go to sleep, they turned on their alarm clock in their bedroom for each child's curfew. When the child came in, they went to the bedroom and shut off their alarm so it wouldn't wake Josef and Sara. For every curfew they came in on time, they got an extra 15 minutes of electronics or television time the following day if they chose to use it. If the children were late and the alarm went off prior to their arrival, then Josef and Sara checked their phones to see if there were messages about the late arrival. If there was a reasonable explanation, then Sara or Josef called Thom or Shannon to validate that things were okay and find out what time they would be returning home. If there was not a text or voicemail from the child, several things would happen: 1) Thom or Shannon got a call from an unhappy parent, 2) the child was grounded for the next 3 days except for required commitments, and 3) for every minute they were late, they lost those late minutes on their next curfew night out. For example, if Thom was 30 minutes late and didn't send a preemptive text or call about why he would be late, then he would lose 30 minutes on his next curfew night out after he was grounded for the next 3 days.

Identify consequences and incentives related to your family expectations and rules, making sure that strategies to reward desirable behavior significantly outweigh the consequences for challenging behavior. Write down your ideas in the following activity and/or complete the Responding to Behavior section of the Family PBS Plan available in the *Helping Your Family Thrive* workbook.

■ ACTIVITY ■ Responding to Behavior

Desirable Behaviors

1. Behavior:

    _____

    _____

    _____

    Consequences:

    _____

    _____

    _____

2. Behavior:

    _____

    _____

    _____

    Consequences:

    _____

    _____

    _____

3. Behavior:

    _____

    _____

    _____

    Consequences:

    _____

    _____

    _____

Undesirable Behaviors

1. Behavior:

    _____

    _____

    _____

Consequences:

_____

_____

_____

2. Behavior:

_____

_____

_____

Consequences:

_____

_____

_____

3. Behavior:

_____

_____

_____

Consequences:

_____

_____

_____

SUMMARY: HOW CAN WE HELP
ALL FAMILY MEMBERS MEET EXPECTATIONS?

It is important not to assume that family members know how to do what they are expected to do. We may need to identify and teach skills that will help them participate more effectively in family life and replace behavioral challenges they may be experiencing. Teaching involves explaining, modeling, reminding, practicing, and providing feedback. Our ultimate goal is to help family members be as independent and self-directed as possible.

Helping family members meet behavioral expectations goes beyond explicitly teaching skills, however. How family members respond to a given behavior can also serve to increase or decrease that behavior. What we get or avoid through our behavior determines whether we will engage in the behavior going forward. It is important that desired behavior be followed by positive outcomes (e.g., praise, special activities, reduced demands). When addressing challenging behavior, it is best to simply withhold positive outcomes or use natural and logical consequences. Consequences for behavior should always be planned and respectful.

BEFORE MOVING ON

- Have you identified skills family members may need to meet the expectations?

- Have you developed a plan for teaching those skills, tailored to their needs?

- What positive outcomes would you like to make available for desired behavior?

- How will you address rule breaking and other challenging behavior effectively?

Monitoring Outcomes and Problem Solving

If you have been completing the activities in this book associated with the areas that you identified as important when you completed your self-assessment, then you now have a Family PBS Plan. The plan should include your family vision; expectations and rules; organization of your household; schedule, routines, and time lines; teaching plans; and preplanned consequences for promoting desirable behavior and discouraging challenging behaviors. Hopefully, you have experienced success as you have put these elements in place.

Yet, no plan works perfectly 100% of the time. To ensure continued success, it is important to monitor outcomes on an ongoing basis and make adjustments as needed. You will also need to be prepared to problem-solve when any unexpected challenges arise, including challenges with individual family members. This chapter guides you in monitoring outcomes and problem solving.

MONITORING AND ADJUSTING YOUR PLAN

We encourage you to revisit Chapter 3 and repeat the Family PBS Self-Check to ensure that your family has experienced success and track your ongoing progress. You should first and foremost celebrate what is working. If you feel you have made mistakes, then forgive yourself. And if you feel you are missing key elements or need to tweak something, now is the time to make changes. You may want to reread specific sections of this book that focus on the areas of concern for your family and go back to the drawing board. It is beneficial to do this kind of self-assessment periodically—maybe every 6 months to a year. If you do, you may find that you have drifted from your original plan or vision or some of your actions no longer align with your stated values. You may also find that your circumstances and needs have changed. This certainly will be the case as children develop and experience new people, places, and activities. Your plan will also need adjustment if your family undergoes a significant event or transition, such as adding a new family member, experiencing a divorce or remarriage, or moving to a new home.

The best laid plans allow for flexibility and adjustment as circumstances change. The process outlined in this book is meant to be adaptable, flexible, and revisited often rather than prescribed or set in stone, as it is common for family and individual needs to shift and change over time. You may not get it quite right the first time, but you will learn what works and what doesn't so you can continually problem-solve as a family, fine-tuning your plan as you go.

In addition to repeating the self-check, hopefully you have been completing the Weekly Family Behavior Rating Tool in Chapter 3 throughout this process. You may now review your data to see if there is objective evidence of changes in how your family functions. This weekly rating has six (or more) items describing positive behaviors and is scored on a 0–3 rating, with 0 being "not at all" and 3 being "always." If you want, you can graph your data from 0 to 18 (which would indicate 3s in all six areas). If your scores are consistently above 12, then you should feel confident that things are going well. If your scores are below 12, then you may need to tweak your plan, problem solving around the areas of concern. If you are really struggling, then your plan may need a major overhaul, or you may need to ask for help or for support beyond your family members. Please note that variability in your ratings is to be expected. We all have difficult periods. Therefore, focus on the overall patterns, rather than one single rating.

The Wagner Family: Tracking Progress and Tweaking the Plan

The Wagners decided to revisit their behavior ratings every 2 weeks for 12 weeks so they could discuss how things were going and make adjustments as needed. The graph in Figure 7.1 shows the family ratings in the six areas over the 12 weeks.

The Wagners felt like their new chore selection process helped divide up the tasks in a much better manner. It took the family several weeks to get into the groove of doing their chores correctly and completely because the kids initially assumed if they didn't do their tasks, Josef or Sara would do them instead. That's when the family started Taco Tuesday as the incentive for everyone to complete their chores on time.

Once the family began discussing their lack of hearing each other around the house, they all made a conscious effort to keep music at more reasonable levels and avoid yelling from room to room. Instead, they agreed to find the person they needed something from and talk to them directly about what was

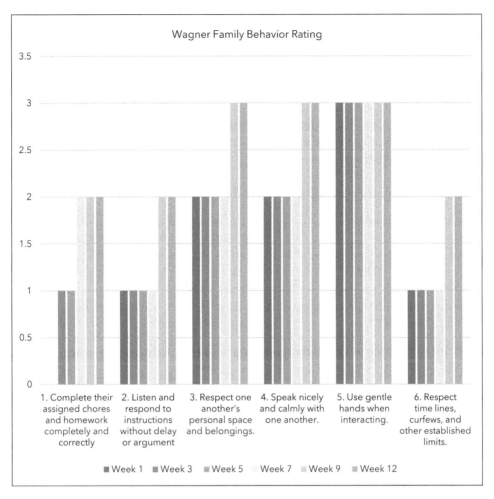

Figure 7.1.   The Wagner family's graph of data for each item on their Weekly Family Behavior Rating, showing scores for weeks 1, 3, 5, 7, 9, and 12.

needed and clarify if someone didn't understand. With reduced frustration and improved communication, yelling went away. The weekly family dinner and meetings allowed them to clarify things such as skills needed to teach family members. With frustrations down as communications became more regular and people's belongings could be found, the yelling in the house went away.

When the storage units by the doors and in the family room started working to keep the house more organized and allow everyone to find their things, Julia asked if they could do something like that in the kids' shared bathroom because finding stuff and having enough time was still a problem. Josef put in two floating shelves while Sara and the girls went to the Dollar Thrift Store and selected a plastic bin for each child's hair, face, and teeth products. The Dollar Thrift Store also had small standing mirrors so each of the girls could do hair and makeup in their bedrooms to free up time for the boys to use the bathroom.

We encourage you to keep using this Weekly Family Behavior Rating Tool. If you find that you are experiencing success with your family plan and completing the tool weekly feels like too much, then you could drop it down to every 2 weeks or once per month. It may be helpful to program reminders into your calendar or complete the rating during regular family meetings. We strongly encourage you to connect with your entire family at least every couple of weeks to reevaluate how you are doing. Take this opportunity to determine what is working and what changes may be needed to ensure that your family plan is effectively supporting everyone.

ADDRESSING BEHAVIOR OF INDIVIDUAL MEMBERS

What do you do if all except one of your family members is responding well to your family plan? Some family members may be less responsive to the structure and routines in your plan. They may even engage in behavior that is unusually oppositional, disruptive, or dangerous. They may be facing unique challenges that significantly affect their behavior. Although these issues might arise sporadically for everyone, longstanding concerns should be addressed. In this case, it may be necessary to gain access to additional resources and/or seek professional assistance from a trained professional (e.g., behavior analyst, psychologist, counselor, clergy) with expertise in the area of concern.

It is beyond the scope of this book to address individualized behavior support in any detail; this topic is outlined extensively in the companion book *Resolving Your Child's Challenging Behavior: A Practical Guide to Parenting With Positive Behavior Support* (Hieneman, Elfner, & Sergay, 2022). In this book, however, we give an overview of the process to provide general guidance for you as you seek appropriate help. One important caveat: PBS is something you do with people, not to people. It should be a collaborative, respectful process to help your family member live a more meaningful and satisfying life. The steps are listed next and described in the following sections:

1. Identify the behaviors of concern and goals for the family member.

2. Look for patterns that might be affecting your family member's behavior.

3. Work together to develop strategies to effectively support the family member's behavior.

4. Put the plan in place and evaluate the outcomes for your family member.

Identify Behaviors of Concern and Goals

Behaviors of concern are actions that a person is either not doing enough (e.g., completing chores or homework) or doing too much (e.g., yelling, threatening, storming out). You want to figure out what exactly your family member is saying or doing that is problematic for them and the rest of the family. It is also important to consider how a change in that behavior could affect the family member's life in general (e.g., finishing high school, maintaining friendships).

Look for Patterns

As previously mentioned, behavior is influenced by what comes before it (antecedents) and what follows it (consequences). Antecedents could include a variety of events, such as being ignored or interrupted, losing a valued item, or being told to do something difficult, arduous, or unpleasant. Consequences that maintain behavior tend to be attention from others; access to preferred activities, events, or items; or delaying, stopping, or preventing unpleasant circumstances. Stepping back from the situation, you may be able to recognize what circumstances tend to provoke the behaviors of concern and what the family member gets, prevents, or stops by their behavior.

Broader events or conditions may also affect a family member. These could include physiological issues, such as lack of sleep, poor eating habits/diet, and illness or allergies, or mental health issues such as depression. They could also include social and motivational issues such as traumatic events, significant changes in routines, relationships ending, increasingly busy and stressful schedules, or major disappointments such as failure at work, school, or in sports. Identifying the circumstances that may contribute to a family member's behavior will help identify possible solutions that are based on understanding.

Work Together to Develop Support Strategies

When you have a good idea of the antecedents, consequences, and broader issues that may be affecting a family member's behavior, you are empowered to generate creative, positive solutions. Strategies fall into four general categories (proactive strategies, teaching strategies, consequence strategies, and broader supports). Proactive strategies address antecedents and focus on preventing problems or helping prompt more desirable behavior. Examples might include changing the way we approach the family member when asking them to do something or removing distracting items when they need to get things done.

Consequence strategies include making sure we make positive outcomes available for desirable behavior and not challenging behavior. We addressed this generally in Chapter 6, but individual-specific examples might include holding on to the controls to video games until work is completed, praising acceptance of consequences, or redirecting attention or no longer responding to continued arguing after a decision has been reached. Teaching strategies align with Chapter 6 and include identifying specific replacement behaviors that allow family members to get attention, items, or activities or lessen or delay demands more appropriately. For example, you might encourage a family member to count to 10 when frustrated, providing time to formulate a calmer message.

In addition to these immediate strategies, broader supports might be needed for a family member to change their behavior. These might include working with them to improve their organizational skills or rearrange their bedroom, play area, or workspace to create a more comfortable, useful, or supportive environment. It might mean addressing medical or psychological issues. Finally, it might involve revisiting aspects of the family plan that are of concern to the family member, making reasonable adjustments.

Put the Plan in Place and Evaluate Outcomes

As with your family plan, you need to make sure everyone is on the same page in supporting the family member who is having difficulty. That way, the strategies can be used more consistently. It may be helpful to keep an individualized record of goal achievement and behaviors of concern (e.g., a daily rating of specific behaviors). The best option is for the family member to track their own behavior, with support from others.

This chapter previously described how the Wagner family monitored their own success with their plan. Overall, life had improved over the past 12 weeks. Family members were using positive behaviors more consistently, as shown by the graph in Figure 7.1. Yet, two family members struggled with specific behaviors—Tristan with throwing toys and Thom with missing curfew and arguing about it.

As you read about how the Wagners addressed Tristan's behavior, think about how they identified goals and analyzed patterns. Notice the strategies they decided on to support the behavior they wanted to see from Tristan and the ways they implemented their plan and evaluated how it was working.

The Wagner Family: Addressing Tristan's Behavior

Although Tristan had been making good progress using "gentle hands" and not hitting or pinching people, throwing toys had gotten worse. He wasn't throwing them at people, but it was definitely a behavior no one in the family liked. Therefore, his family talked about how to get this corrected. The family agreed that the desired behavior was for Tristan to set toys down nicely in an appropriate place. They considered the possible reasons (or functions) for his behavior. They noticed that Tristan seemed excited by the noise and movement of toys going through the air and then striking. They also noticed that they tended to react to Tristan's behavior by telling him to stop and sometimes yelling. The parents explained and showed Tristan which toys (e.g., balls outside) were okay to throw and gave him toys he could use inside that made noises. They decided to start responding to Tristan using toys nicely by saying, "It looks like you are having fun with that toy" or "Thank you for setting your toy down/away nicely" whenever anyone saw him using them correctly. Instead of reacting to Tristan throwing, the family member who saw the toy being thrown would say "Uh-oh, Tristan, we use toys nicely. The toy is now gone for 2 days," and they put the toy on the off-limits shelf. If Tristan didn't throw a toy for an entire day, then he got a toy down from the off-limits shelf to play with during his before dinner play time and they told him, "Tristan, you used your toys nicely for a whole day, so you earned a toy back." If Tristan threw a toy and it broke, then that was the natural consequence and it was thrown in the trash. The family member would say, "Uh-oh, the toy doesn't work anymore because it's broken. This is why we don't throw toys, Tristan. We set them down nicely so they don't get broken." They decided to keep a tally of each time Tristan threw his toys to make sure the behavior was decreasing over time.

The Wagners followed the same broad steps to address Thom's behavior—identifying the concern and goal, analyzing patterns, determining supports, putting the plan in place, and evaluating outcomes. The way they followed these steps was different, however, given the nature of the behavior and Thom's age. As you read, think about why they chose the strategies they used with Thom and how these strategies may help Thom to learn how to manage the increasing independence of adolescence.

The Wagner Family: Addressing Thom's Behavior

Although the family had rules and consequences associated with curfews, Thom continued his verbal pushback against his curfew, which was beginning to result in him calling all the time saying he was going to be late before the alarm clock went off. His curfew was later when he was at his mom's house, so Josef and Sara sat down with Kat to see how it was working. Kat said she had been having some of the same issues when Thom had an earlier curfew at her house. Kat and David spoke with other parents of 16-year-old boys about their curfew times and decided to try a later curfew for Thom on the condition he no longer would argue about what time they set, and if he was late even once, they would revert to the earlier curfew for 2 weeks again. They told Thom he needed to demonstrate personal responsibility with the later time. They had made the change 3 months ago, and Thom had never missed his curfew since, nor was he arguing about the time any longer. Josef and Sara decided to set the same new curfew times for Thom at their house, with the same conditions in place. Thom has since shown the same respect for the new curfew at their house, and the entire family noticed this improvement in their week 9 and 12 ratings.

SUMMARY: HOW CAN WE KEEP OUR FAMILY ON TRACK?

PBS is not a one-and-done approach. It involves ongoing monitoring and problem solving. With objective information from the Weekly Family Behavior Rating Tool and Family PBS Self-Check, you can celebrate your successes and tweak your strategies to achieve the best possible results for your family.

Hopefully, your family members will all buy-in to your plan and enjoy the process. Sometimes, however, individual members experience resistance or challenging behavior that needs special attention. If this occurs, PBS provides a problem-solving process by which you identify goals and behaviors of concern, gather information and analyze patterns, and develop, implement, and monitor individualized plans. More information about this process may be found in *Resolving Your Child's Challenging Behavior: A Practical Guide to Parenting With Positive Behavior Support* (Hieneman, Elfner, & Sergay, 2022).

BEFORE MOVING ON

- Is a member of your family having difficulty responding to your family plan?

- If so, have you used the problem-solving process in this chapter or consulted other sources (e.g., books, professionals) to develop more effective strategies?

- Have you identified skills family members may need to meet the expectations?

- Have you developed a plan for teaching those skills, tailored to their needs?

Making It Work

As you and your family have been working through the steps outlined in this book, there may have been points when you wanted to say, "Yes, but . . ." These "buts" may have been due to interpersonal or situational challenges that are unique to your family. In this section, we address some of the variables that are likely to affect a family's adoption of PBS approaches. We also share two case examples that illustrate how PBS may be tailored to families with different characteristics and needs.

8

Building Family Processes to Promote Success

Family life can be complex and challenging. Difficulties can arise, affecting interpersonal communication, increasing stress levels, restricting the supports available, or even damaging the cohesiveness of your family. When such difficulties are severe, it is often beneficial to seek assistance from a skilled and objective outsider (e.g., counselor, clergy). Although it is not the focus of this book to go into each of these topics in detail, we describe these issues in this chapter. We provide some general tips regarding how to enhance available social and emotional support, thereby increasing your ability to fully engage in a family PBS process. These tips include:

- Communicating more effectively
- Maintaining strong family relationships
- Participating in community life and activities
- Managing stress and negativity
- Strengthening family unity

Each of these issues should be considered within your family's unique characteristics, including your culture and community, as well as family traditions, norms, and values.

DOWNLOADABLE RESOURCES

You may find the following resource from the *Helping Your Family Thrive* workbook helpful as you read this chapter and complete the activities:

- Family PBS Plan (Making It Work section)

Visit the Brookes Download Hub to obtain this resource for Chapter 8.

COMMUNICATING EFFECTIVELY

Communication includes how we listen and how we express ourselves with words, expressions, or gestures. Communication is essential in PBS because mixed messages can break down any family interaction. Author Stephen Covey (1997) said that we should always "seek first to understand, then to be understood" (p. 201) and emphasized that empathetic communication is essential for problem solving as a family. Listening is important for all family members, but it is a skill that may be easy to overlook. Listening means remaining quiet and attentive when other people are talking. It involves avoiding assumptions and second-guessing of motives, and, instead, asking questions to gain a complete understanding of what another person is saying. To listen effectively, you need to put down what you are doing and focus. If that is not possible at the moment, then you should arrange a time and place when you can give your family your full attention (e.g., "I have to wrap up this email by 5:00. Can we talk then?").

Communication also includes how we express ourselves to others. You need to make sure the other person is attentive and you provide a clear message. Your message may include sharing your thoughts or feelings about a situation, relaying important information, or asking something of the other person. Consider the language you are using, as well as your tone and body language, when expressing yourself. For example, if you are suggesting or offering choices, then your communication will be different than if you are telling a family member that something needs to be done. Positivity and respect are always important in communication. It can be helpful to first validate or restate the other person's feelings to ensure that they feel heard and understood before inserting your message (e.g., "I can tell that you are frustrated and want to play with this toy. First it's your brothers turn, then you will get to play again").

Try to avoid communication roadblocks such as criticizing, threatening, or using sarcasm during your most frustrating moments. Using I-messages when communicating about frustrations can be a helpful way to combat these potential pitfalls. Yelling is a common response and can become habitual because it is often a stress reliever. Defensiveness interferes with conflict resolution. If you find that you or other family members default to these and other unproductive types of communication, then you may want to explore ways to build new skills to decrease these habits, possibly using stress management strategies addressed later in this chapter. It is important to recognize that each family member's ability to listen and communicate effectively may be different. Some members may need more time to process information or more direct, detailed instructions. Effective communication—listening and expressing—is especially important when faced with important decisions or resolving problems.

MAINTAINING STRONG RELATIONSHIPS

It is much easier to plan and resolve problems together when interpersonal relationships among family members are strong. Some family members can find themselves falling into the dictator trap in which communications are limited to telling others what to do or asking when it will get done. Nagging can cause other family members to tune out and can lead to resistance, avoidance, and power struggles over time. Relationships may also be plagued with other types of negativity, such as patterns of teasing and intimidation, which can damage relationships. The good news is that counteracting problematic interaction patterns and building emotional collateral is easy. Negativity can often be reversed by deliberately looking for desirable traits and behaviors of others and expressing gratitude. It can also be reduced by engaging in mutually enjoyable activities. If you find yourself at odds with another family member, then think about what you love about them and share your feelings or schedule a special quality time with them.

Sometimes relationship problems stem from unresolved conflict. If that is the case, then the conflict should not be left to fester. Effective conflict resolution requires open communication in which you define the problem, share your feelings and perspectives, brainstorm possible solutions, and make a commitment to change. Family members often come to recognize they have done something hurtful or made a mistake, whether intentional or unintentional, through this process. If so, a sincere, heartfelt apology can go a long way to improving the relationship.

PARTICIPATING IN COMMUNITY LIFE

It is not uncommon for families who are struggling interpersonally to pull back and isolate themselves. This is typically not beneficial because our social circles and community lives give us energy and purpose. Engagement outside the home may give family members a reprieve from household demands and an opportunity to exert their independence. Therefore, healthy families tend to promote friendships, connections with extended family, and maintenance of other support systems. They also encourage participation in activities family members value, such as sports, leisure, clubs, and civic activities. It is important to periodically ask yourself and other family members whether you are doing things that are important to you and seeing people you enjoy on a regular basis. If not, those activities should be prioritized and supported by your family (and put on the family calendar).

MANAGING STRESS AND NEGATIVITY

Anxiety, frustration, and discouragement can interfere with family members' consistency in following even the best-laid plan. For this reason, it is important to consider both external and internal sources of stress. External sources come from the demands of daily life, including stressful jobs or ridiculously busy schedules, financial pressures, or transitions (e.g., changing schools, moving). It may be overwhelming to try to balance everyone's needs when faced with these external stressors. The best way for you to deal with such issues is to problem-solve and determine where and how you can make changes to relieve or simplify the demands, create better organizational systems, or delegate tasks to someone else.

Internal sources of stress derive from your thoughts and feelings. Family members may be discouraged or overwhelmed, thinking that things are generally terrible or will never improve. These thoughts can lead to hypervigilance or despair. Professional help may be warranted when these thoughts are persistent or all encompassing. Stress can have physiological effects such as increased heart rate, muscle tension, and shortness of breath. Feeling overwhelmed or sad is not unusual in families, especially those with complex needs.

Family members can use approaches such as optimism training and mindfulness practice to manage stress. Optimism training is a way of recognizing and replacing unproductive thoughts. Engaging with the world with an optimistic lens involves challenging negative self-talk and learning how to 1) consider bad things as temporary and good things as permanent and lasting, 2) internalize and take credit for positive events and depersonalize the causes of negative events, and 3) allow positive events to enhance all areas of life while considering failures as domain specific. For more information on optimism, see Durand's (2011) *Optimistic Parenting: Hope and Help for You and Your Challenging Child* and/or Seligman's (2006) *Learned Optimism: How to Change Your Mind and Your Life*. Mindfulness practices help family members connect to the moment, find acceptance, let go of worries, and focus on their intentions. Mindfulness is about learning how to be fully present and nonjudgmental and can be helpful to ensure that family members are fully attending to one another, noticing their own feelings, pausing before reacting or responding, and staying open to different perspectives. To use these practices, you need to consider what situations tend to produce stress, what you think and feel in those moments, how your thoughts and feelings translate into action, and how you might reframe your thinking and/or reduce stress in the moment. It is also helpful to find ways to fill your bucket through self-care. If you enjoy taking long walks, hanging out with friends, binge-watching episodes of your favorite programs, surfing the Internet, getting massages, reading trashy novels, or taking long showers or bubble baths, then these can help center you when things get difficult. As Randy Pausch said in the Last Lecture, put your oxygen mask on first before trying to assist others. For more about mindfulness, see Race's (2014) *Mindful Parenting: Simple and Powerful Solutions for Raising Creative, Engaged, Happy Kids in Today's Hectic World* and/or the Kabat-Zinns' (2014) *Everyday Blessings: The Inner Work of Mindful Parenting*.

STRENGTHENING FAMILY UNITY

Creating a Family PBS Plan and addressing any needs discovered in the preceding sections of this chapter can contribute to family unity. It is, however, important to consider how you can strengthen and maintain your bonds. Families are often held together by traditions and rituals. Throughout the book, we have encouraged having regular family meetings to talk about how things are going and resolve problems together. This is very important because it keeps lines of communication open. Most families have other traditions they value, including conversation starters at family dinners, movie or game nights, religious or spiritual activities, or rituals associated with holidays and birthdays. Family projects can also strengthen togetherness as you tackle challenges and have fun together. The ways we communicate, interact, deal with stress, and maintain family bonds are, of course, shaped by our culture and values. Each family should tailor their approaches to what is right for their family.

The Wagner Family: Fine-Tuning for Communication and Consistency

Through this process, the Wagner Family improved their communication and consistency. The family meetings gave them the consistent outlet they needed for schedule planning to reduce family stress and confusion. Josef and Sara decided to further structure the meetings to share more about individual family members' lives and stay connected to their vision. At each meal, they did a round table in which each member answered these questions: 1) What is going great for you this week? 2) What is something you are finding challenging this week, and who or what could help you address the challenge? 3) Can you think of anything we need to do differently in our home or as individuals to better meet our vision? They made a decorative plaque with their vision: *The Wagners put family first, and we are responsible, kind, and honest to each other and within our community.*

These weekly conversations allowed all members to celebrate successes and pleasant events and to prompt problem solving. The family members were able to guide the choices and felt more included in one another's lives. It was also an opportunity to express gratitude for the support they were getting and determine whether responsibilities should be increased, decreased, or changed.

The family had structures in place for weekly game/playtime, which helped with family unity, and they regularly supported each other by attending school events, soccer games, and Thom's band practices and performances. In addition, the family started volunteering at their local food shelter for food drives in the community and during some holidays.

In addition to the internal family communications, Sara and Josef reached out more to school teachers and family to support and improve their consistent use of PBS. In particular, they often relied on Melanie (Josef's and Sara's sister-in-law) for an objective perspective and guidance. They shared the way they were holding Tristan accountable to treat his toys nicely with both his preschool teachers and the other family members who watched him. Sara scheduled a team meeting with Julia's teachers and therapists to show them how to use the *First-Then Visual Scheduler* and asked them all to think about routines or tasks that could be added to the application. They also discussed what activities they could combine with music as Julia's use of headphones was a very calming tool for her in loud and even in bright spaces.

Sara came to recognize that her stress level often contributed to challenges in the household. When she was feeling overwhelmed, she tended to get hypervigilant, ordering people around and becoming consumed with unimportant details. Therefore, she decided to take 15 minutes each morning before the rest of the family awoke to sit on her back porch, listen to wind chimes, and ground herself before starting the day. Josef and Shannon developed similar routines after they saw the affect that this mindfulness practice had on Sara.

The Wagner family felt their personal use of PBS has not only improved their communications internally, but it also made them more thoughtful in how they share and communicate with their broader family, friends, and community.

To fine-tune your own family plan, complete the following Making It Work activity. (A full-size, fillable PDF version is available in the downloadable *Helping Your Family Thrive* workbook.)

■ ACTIVITY ■ Making It Work

As a family, reflect on each of the following areas and identify things you can do to strengthen your family, thereby using your family plan more consistently.

Communicating effectively

_____

_____

_____

_____

_____

Maintaining strong relationships

_____

_____

_____

_____

_____

Participating in community life

_____

_____

_____

_____

_____

Managing stress and negativity

_____

_____

_____

_____

_____

Strengthening family unity

_____

_____

_____

_____

_____

SUMMARY: HOW CAN WE FURTHER STRENGTHEN OUR FAMILY?

There are certain requisites to the success of PBS in families. Families who effectively communicate with one another, maintain strong relationships, participate in social and community activities, manage their stress, and work to strengthen family unity tend to succeed and live happier, more fulfilled lives.

BEFORE MOVING ON

- Have you identified any larger issues that might affect your family's ability to fully participate in the PBS process?

- If so, what steps can you take to address or overcome these issues?

The Denison Family

This chapter shares the story of the Denison family. First, we describe the family's composition, strengths, challenges, and status before starting the PBS process. Next, we guide you through the family's approach to developing their vision and expectations; adapting their environment, schedule, and routines; teaching and encouraging desired behavior; and monitoring progress and adjusting their plan. The chapter concludes with considerations for broad, long-term support. Throughout this chapter, we ask you to reflect on "What do you think?" questions to consider how you would apply PBS in the Denison family's situation.

ABOUT THE DENISONS

The Denison family lives in a two-bedroom apartment between a bustling city and the suburbs. Reanna (Mom) has primary custody of their two boys—Marcus (13) and Liam (11). Reanna, Marcus, and Liam have been mostly on their own since Reanna's divorce when the boys were 3 and 5. The boys' father (Damon) calls them every week or so and visits roughly twice per year. Damon sometimes sends expensive gifts or plans special outings when his landscaping business is going well. Damon is not involved in day-to-day decision making, leaving those choices to Reanna. The boys look up to Damon because he is attentive and generous during their visits. Reanna is very close to her mother, Allie, often talking with her on the phone several times per week. Allie is a retired teacher. Allie sometimes criticizes Reanna's parenting and feels frustrated that she cannot help more because she lives 5 hours away. Reanna's primary local support systems are her church family and a couple of neighbors.

Reanna works as a reservation agent for a large hotel chain. She spends 8 or more hours on the computer per day, with only short breaks. Marcus and Liam attend the same middle school, which is within walking distance of their home. Reanna often jokes that Marcus and Liam are attached at the hip. They share the same humor and music preferences and are usually on the same side of any issue. They enjoy planning activities and completing projects together and are always willing to pitch in if Reanna asks them to help. When not at school, the boys spend their time playing video games or hanging out at the community park.

The boys have recently been getting into trouble in the neighborhood. They have been accused of swearing in front of younger children, breaking light fixtures, and doorbell-ditching the neighbors, all of which they deny. Marcus and Liam's school requested to meet with Reanna because both boys' grades have been slipping, putting them at risk of retention next year. The teachers were kind and supportive, but they emphasized that the boys needed more supervision and support at home to succeed. They explained that PBS had been helpful at their school and suggested that the same principles could be applied at home. Reanna searched the term online and found this book. Although it seemed a bit complicated at first, Allie and school staff said they would be happy to help.

STATUS BEFORE BEGINNING PROCESS

The first step in the PBS process was for Reanna and her boys to evaluate how they were doing as a family to determine what they currently had in place, as well as their strengths and challenges. When Reanna tried to get the boys to sit down and work with her on the ratings, they initially made silly jokes and distracted one another. Reanna decided that pizza would be necessary. She told the boys if they helped her answer the questions, then they could order pizza for dinner. After identifying various strengths and challenges (see Figure 9.1), Reanna read each question on the Weekly Family Behavior Rating Tool aloud and asked them to rate how often each behavior occurred. They shared examples and nonexamples and eventually agreed on the initial ratings (see Figure 9.2). By filling out this rating, Reanna and the boys recognized that they were typically kind to one another and helpful. The boys would periodically hassle over their games, borrow clothing without asking, or get into wrestling matches that could escalate to someone getting injured (e.g., bruise, scrape), but these did not happen often. They acknowledged that their most significant challenges were related to the boys completing their homework and Reanna delegating chores when she was overwhelmed. Whereas Marcus and Liam did not see it as a major concern, Reanna realized that the boys had a great deal of unstructured time, with limited accountability for their actions.

Considering these broad concerns, Reanna decided to journal about their best and worst times, hoping to better understand the circumstances contributing to their family behavior. The journal entry shown in Figure 9.3 provides examples of these patterns, noting common events during school afternoons and weekends.

Denison **Family**	
Members: *Reanna, Marcus, and Liam (plus Allie and Damon)*	
Strengths	**Challenges**
• *Reanna has a full-time job with good pay.* • *Reanna's mother Allie is willing to offer support.* • *Marcus and Liam like to be busy and help.* • *The boys have a good relationship with their Dad.* • *Church family and neighbors are available.* • *School is offering assistance, rather than blaming the problems on Reanna.*	• *Reanna tends to try to handle everything on her own instead of accepting help.* • *Damon's extravagant gifts and outings can undermine Reanna's limits.* • *Allie criticizes Reanna's parenting and lives too far to help with the boys.* • *Marcus and Liam are performing poorly in school and getting into trouble.*

Figure 9.1.   The Denison family's Strengths and Challenges worksheet.

Reanna found journaling in this way to be very helpful. She realized that Saturdays tend to be structured, and her time with the boys was crucial in keeping them on track. By contrast, weekday afternoons were not mapped out, and Marcus and Liam had little guidance or oversight. Reanna realized that she was unable to keep them on track with her current work schedule.

Over another pizza, Reanna and the boys completed the Family PBS Self-Check (see Figure 9.4). They used the same process as they did with the Weekly Family Behavior Rating Tool, taking more time to consider each item and discuss their many strengths as well as the missing elements of PBS that could have been contributing to the challenges they were facing.

Going through the Family PBS Self-Check was eye opening for Reanna and the boys. They felt good about their relationships with one another, but they also realized that they tended to rely only on one another. They would discuss problems as they arose, but there were no clear expectations, limits, and rules, leading to miscommunication. They kept their home organized, but sometimes Reanna was unable to keep track of where the boys were and what they were doing. They realized that they would need to work together to get more consistency.

Weekly Family Behavior Rating	Never	Sometimes	Usually	Always
Family members complete their assigned chores (and homework) completely and correctly.	0	(1)	2	3
Family members listen and respond to instructions without delay or argument.	0	1	2	(3)
Family members respect one another's personal space and belongings.	0	1	(2)	3
Family members speak nicely and calmly with one another (e.g., no insults, name calling).	0	1	2	(3)
Family members use gentle hands when interacting (i.e., no physical aggression).	0	1	(2)	3
Family members respect time lines, curfews, and other established limits.	0	(1)	2	3
Other (personal behavioral goals for your family)	0	1	2	3

Figure 9.2. The Denisons' Weekly Family Behavior Rating Tool.

■ WHAT DO YOU THINK? ■

Given this family's strengths and challenges, what supports do you think they need to improve their family functioning?

_____

_____

_____

_____

_____

_____

Family Interaction Journal		
At Our Best: Successful or Enjoyable Activity		
What was happening before and around us (e.g., activity)?	What did we each say or do?	How did everyone react, and what was the result?
Everyone sleeps in a bit because it is the weekend. Reanna gets up first and makes a to-do list for the day. The apartment needs some care, but the day is wide open otherwise.	*Marcus and Liam get up, dressed, and ready on their own. Reanna prepares one of their favorite breakfasts. They all sit down to eat together. Reanna talks about what needs to get done around the apartment, and the boys commit to helping. They work together, joking as they complete the tasks.*	*Reanna and the boys look around and see how much they have accomplished. They decide to throw the football around to get some fresh air and exercise.*
At Our Worst: Challenging or Frustrating Activity		
What was happening before and around us (e.g., activity)?	What did we each say or do?	How did everyone react, and what was the result?
Reanna is busy at work on her computer, juggling new reservations and emails from her boss about productivity goals. The boys come home from school. They wave to Reanna and then head to the kitchen.	*Marcus and Liam raid the fridge and then talk about what they want to do this afternoon. They play video games for 30 minutes and head to the neighborhood park. Twenty minutes later, they come running back in, laughing. Reanna wonders what they have been doing, but cannot leave the computer.*	*A neighbor comes to the door, complaining that Marcus and Liam have been picking on other kids and running amok in the neighborhood. The boys once again do not complete their homework.*

Figure 9.3. The Denisons' Family Interaction Journal.

Family PBS Self-Check

Family name: *Denison*

Member(s) responding: *Reanna, Marcus, Liam*   Date: *12/3*

Please rate the degree that each the following are in place by checking the appropriate column.

Family Vision and Expectations	Not at all	Somewhat	Very much	Notes
Shared values and goals		✓		*We share values and boys pitch in, but expectations and rules aren't clear.*
Clear behavioral expectations	✓			
Rules regarding misbehavior	✓			
Household responsibilities			✓	
Organization of Space and Time	**Not at all**	**Somewhat**	**Very much**	**Notes**
Good household organization		✓		*We don't have regular routines/ calendar. We communicate, and boys have a regular bedtime.*
Shared family calendar	✓			
Consistent daily routines	✓			
Notice of schedule changes		✓		
Time limits on activities		✓		
Teaching and Basic Discipline	**Not at all**	**Somewhat**	**Very much**	**Notes**
Explaining and modeling		✓		*We are kind and supportive but do not have consistent consequences.*
Praise for positive behavior			✓	
Privileges linked to behavior	✓			
Pre-planned consequences	✓			
Respectful discipline methods			✓	
Supporting Family Life	**Not at all**	**Somewhat**	**Very much**	**Notes**
Open, clear communication		✓		*Our relationships are positive, but sometimes we do not share things and we stay to ourselves a lot.*
General respect and kindness			✓	
Effective problem resolution		✓		
Strong, loving relationships			✓	
Ability to manage stress		✓		
Support of family and friends		✓		
Full community participation		✓		

Figure 9.4.   The Denisons' Family PBS Self-Check.

FAMILY VISION AND EXPECTATIONS

The next step was to develop a vision based on the family's values. Reanna realized that she had never taken the time to consider this, operating mostly on her instincts. Feeling a little lost, Reanna called her mother and asked what values drove their household. Allie explained that her value to contribute to society and stay connected is what held them together. When Reanna asked the boys to discuss their values, they immediately started making jokes. Reanna waited them out, and they eventually joined in the discussion. As they talked, they realized that they had pulled together following a difficult divorce. They believed in loyalty, acceptance, cooperation, and appreciation. Marcus and Liam acknowledged that they liked the freedom to do their own thing. Reanna explained that she had always believed in hard work and perseverance and that those values had become increasingly important as the boys had gotten older. They agreed that responsibility and accountability were important, but their motto (or vision) had always been "Together, we can achieve anything."

■ WHAT DO YOU THINK? ■

Given the vision and priorities of this family, what behavioral expectations do you think would be important for them?

_____

_____

_____

_____

_____

_____

With these values and mission in mind, the Denisons discussed behavioral expectations, rules, and limits to help them stay aligned with their vision. They wanted to continue to focus on what worked for them but also add new expectations. Here is what they created:

Be kind, helpful, and appreciative of one another.

Be responsible, doing what you have to do first.

Be accountable for your actions and whereabouts.

These very simple expectations naturally led to rules and time lines. The rules included the following:

1. Homework and chores must be done prior to leaving the house or playing video games every weekday afternoon.

2. To continue to have freedom, you must communicate where you are going and be accountable for your actions.

3. Disrespectful or destructive behavior will result in increased supervision.

Because Marcus and Liam had not been doing well academically or behaviorally at school, Reanna decided to take the school up on their offer to use a daily behavior rating. That tool would provide regular feedback on whether the boys completed their work and abided by the school rules. Although they decided not to adopt the school's expectations (BEARS: Be responsible, Engage in learning, Act safely, Respect yourself and others, Show a positive attitude) in their entirety, Reanna knew that supporting those expectations at home was very important.

■ WHAT DO YOU THINK? ■

Given the background information on this family, what changes might be helpful in their household, schedule, and routines?

_____

_____

_____

_____

_____

_____

ARRANGING SPACE AND TIME

Next, Reanna and the boys took a close look at their household, schedule, and routines to support their expectations. Their home was usually well maintained, but the boys' homework supplies were all over the place and the video games and controls were in plain sight. Reanna decided to create a designated drawer for pens, pencils, paper, calculators, and other school supplies close to the kitchen table where she wanted Marcus and Liam to do their homework. They also agreed to set up a check-out system for the video game controls. Reanna kept them in her workspace in her bedroom until the boys showed them their completed work. If the boys were going to go to the park or friends' houses, then they had to write down their plans on a sticky note and post it on the refrigerator.

Reanna realized that she could not provide sufficient supervision for the boys while she was working. Therefore, Reanna spoke with her supervisor and asked to have her 15-minute break when the boys arrived home. She could then ask about their day, see what homework they needed to do, and help them make a plan for the rest of the day. Reanna was concerned that there were times the boys needed help with their homework, but she was not available. Because Allie was retired and wanted to help, she offered to be available via an online meeting each afternoon to guide the boys as needed. Although Reanna wanted to trust her sons, she had received several reports of them being disrespectful in the neighborhood. Therefore, Reanna asked the parents of children who she knew had their children at the park regularly to share any concerns with her so that she could address them quickly. Reanna created a text group with the mothers in the neighborhood, and they soon started sharing anecdotes, reports, and updates about their children. She also committed to do spot checks when the boys went to the park on the weekend, bringing them water or snacks while also making sure they behaved as expected.

The boys told Reanna they were often bored, which was probably contributing to their neighborhood trouble. She realized that a lot of children their age participated in sports or clubs. The boys said that they would love to play football. Reanna found a league in which both boys could play on the same team, making the schedule manageable for her. Joining football added two evening practices and one game every Saturday to their schedule, which further structured their time. Reanna also wanted to continue the positive routines she felt led to their closeness as a family. One of these routines was their nighttime talks as they settled down for the evening. They would share their best, worst, and funniest experiences from the day. They decided to keep the schedule loose on weekends, allowing them to relax and enjoy one another's company.

◼ WHAT DO YOU THINK? ◼

How might the skills this family felt needed to be developed be taught and reinforced? How might you deal with behavior that violates family expectations?

_____

_____

_____

_____

_____

TEACHING BEHAVIORAL EXPECTATIONS

As Reanna and the boys added structure to their routines and clarified expectations, they realized there were skills they needed to learn to succeed. Reanna became aware that her biggest challenge was accepting help offered by other people. She would often say, "No, I've got it," even when she was completely slammed with other responsibilities. Instead of immediately refusing help,

Reanna decided to pause, evaluate the offer, determine if it would help, and accept when reasonable. She began ride-sharing with other parents to football practices as well as accepting help from her mother and neighbors with the boys' afternoon routines.

Marcus and Liam were terrific about pitching in around the house. They usually cleaned up after themselves, took out the trash, put their clothes away, and even cleaned the kitchen and bathroom when asked to help their mother. They did not, however, enjoy those chores. Both boys said they wanted to cook sometimes. Therefore, Reanna taught them how to find and follow recipes and use the kitchen appliances. They picked a recipe each week, Reanna got the necessary ingredients, and Marcus and Liam prepared the meal with whatever guidance they needed from Reanna. Over time, they became more proficient, independent, and adventurous. In addition to learning to cook, Allie (Grandma) worked on project planning and study skills with Marcus and Liam, helping them become more efficient in completing their homework.

As Reanna learned more about positive reinforcement, she noted that she has always praised, thanked, and encouraged Marcus and Liam. She knew that they appreciated the way she supported them, but they tended to look more to their father for approval. Although Reanna had never come in the way of the boys' relationship with Damon, she had never actively encouraged or supported it. Reanna decided to put her ego aside and contacted Damon. Reanna explained that Marcus and Liam were not doing well in school, and they were concerned about their behavior in the neighborhood. She told Damon about the expectations and routines they established, including the boys starting football. Reanna also told Damon about the daily behavior ratings from school. Reanna requested that Damon ask the boys about their achievements at school and in football and praise their positive efforts. She also asked that Damon consider giving gifts only when the boys were doing well (e.g., at the end of quarters when the boys got mostly As and Bs), rather than more arbitrarily. Finally, Reanna asked that Damon hold them accountable for the expectations during his visits. Damon was flattered that she asked for his help and was relieved to know exactly what he could do to be supportive.

Reanna also talked with Marcus and Liam about the reports of their misbehavior at school and the park. In addition to tracking the school's behavior rating, she would also be talking with their teachers and checking in with the neighbors. Because Reanna and the boys had always had an open, respectful relationship, she did not want to be punitive if the boys did something wrong. Instead, Reanna explained that with freedom comes responsibility—the boys could continue to come and go freely, provided they were home for dinner and let her know if they were going to change location. If, however, trusted adults reported that the boys engaged in challenging behavior or they were not where they said they would be, then their freedom would decrease and supervision would increase. The level of restriction would be dependent on the severity of the problem, ranging from just having to be home an hour earlier to not being able to leave the house without Reanna.

■ WHAT DO YOU THINK? ■

Given what you have learned about this family, how might they monitor their interactions and address challenges as they arise?

_____

_____

_____

_____

_____

_____

MONITORING OUTCOMES AND PROBLEM SOLVING

Reanna, Marcus, and Liam did daily check-ins using the school's daily behavior rating. In addition, Reanna felt it would help to sit down every month to repeat their Weekly Family Behavior Rating Tool, review their family expectations, and consider how the changes they had put in place were working. They held their check-in on the first Sunday of each month after church. They noted successes, discussed any challenges they were facing, and planned how they could overcome them. Reanna realized she needed to keep her mother Allie and ex-husband Damon in the loop. She started emailing them each week to provide status reports and open up a dialogue, welcoming input from Allie and Damon. Reanna also responded regularly to the communications from the school staff, keeping everyone working together.

Through these efforts, Marcus and Liam's grades and reports on their behavior improved at school. They became starters on the football team. Because of their leadership roles, they took their reputations more seriously, trying to be role models for younger children on the team and in the neighborhood. Reanna found her stress had decreased considerably, and she had more time to herself. Because the family had pulled together, it was not necessary to address any individual challenges in any systematic way. Instead, even when Marcus missed curfew and Liam decided to harass a neighbor's dog by barking at it repeatedly, they were able to discuss the behavior and apply logical consequences (i.e., Marcus accepting an earlier curfew for 1 week, Liam apologizing to the neighbor and offering to walk the dog).

MAKING IT WORK

This PBS process was helpful for the Denison family. Not only were they able to clarify expectations, improve routines, and increase accountability, but they also found they had grown even closer as a family. Reanna, Marcus, and Liam still enjoyed their down time in the evenings and weekends and further enjoyed coming together around football games and family meetings. Reanna came to realize she had isolated herself in parenting instead of inviting others in to help. Allie was no longer frustrated at her inability to help and bragged to her friends that she was teaching her grandchildren online. Damon followed through with Reanna's requests, feeling confident he was guiding his sons in the right direction and making a positive difference in their lives. Through this process, Reanna became aware that she had been putting everyone's needs above her own and was not taking care of her own health. Reanna decided to start walking the track around the football field each evening when practice was going on and joined an exercise class at her church on Saturday mornings while the boys were still sleeping. Reanna now felt she could more effectively balance her roles as a professional and parent and take care of herself.

10 The Sanchez Family

This chapter outlines the story of the Sanchez family's journey with PBS. First, we describe the family, their strengths and challenges, and how they became engaged in the PBS process. Then we walk through the family planning process they used to develop a family vision and expectations, modifications to their time and space, and methods to promote desired behavior and discourage challenging behaviors among all family members. We wrap up by describing how the family brought the plan together and then monitored and made adjustments to get the best possible outcomes. The Sanchez family provides an excellent example of a multigenerational application of PBS in the home to improve the quality of life for everyone involved. If you want practice with the PBS process, then a "What do you think?" prompt guides you to consider how you might apply each step with the Sanchez family.

ABOUT THE SANCHEZES

The Sanchez family includes Roberto (Dad), Catherine (Mom), and their two young children Alex (4) and Rachel (2), as well as Catherine's mother, Hannah (Grandma). Catherine and Roberto moved from Louisiana to a small New England town 8 years ago for Catherine's job at a local university. Five years ago, they purchased an old four-bedroom farmhouse with help from Hannah, which aligned with their plans to grow their family and have space for relatives as needed. Most of their relatives remain in Louisiana, with their closest family members located in Delaware—an 8-hour drive from their home.

Catherine is a college professor. Her schedule varies from semester to semester, but she typically works from about 8:00 a.m. to 6:30 p.m. and may resume her work after the children are in bed to answer emails and grade assignments. Roberto works part time (25 hours/week) in the early mornings and mostly on weekends at a local café. They arranged what they call a "two ships passing in the night" schedule to accommodate for illnesses, appointments, or other caregiving responsibilities for their family members and reduce child care costs. Catherine is an intellectual introvert who is very focused on goals and accomplishments. Roberto is a gregarious extrovert who lives in the moment.

Hannah came to visit from Louisiana a year ago and has lived with the Sanchez family ever since. She unexpectedly had to remain due to her progressing symptoms of Alzheimer's disease and other family members' inability to care for Hannah. She was a professor like Catherine and is a doting yet hypervigilant mother and grandmother.

Alex was diagnosed with autism spectrum disorder before the age of 2. He receives 20–30 hours of intensive home and school-based applied behavior analysis (ABA) and speech/language services. The ABA services are delivered by a team of behavioral professionals (i.e., behavior analyst, behavior technicians) and involve therapy to teach Alex communication and other skills, as well as improve his behavior. Alex has made excellent progress (including the ability to ask and respond to rapid-fire questions about astronomy and biology); Alex is now able to effectively communicate his wants and needs, as well as be successful in an inclusive preschool setting. Rachel is an expressive toddler who demonstrates a full continuum of emotions and loves to explore. She is most interested in whatever Alex is doing and does not like to leave Catherine's side. The Sanchez family also includes a dog, a cat, and a Venus flytrap plant that requires feeding.

Although their personalities differ, Catherine and Roberto share similar values around the importance of family. They work well together in terms of division of household labor and collaborative decision making. Both Catherine and Roberto have a loving network of friends and family throughout the country and have close relationships with their colleagues. Catherine and Roberto feel they can typically count on one another for support and empathy. They both have jobs they enjoy and at which they excel. They share a commitment to doing everything they can for Hannah, Alex, and Rachel and are quite patient. They are "systems savvy" because they can navigate complex health care, education, and medical insurance processes to gain access to services to support their family's needs. Hannah serves as a caring listening ear to both of them and helps with household tasks such as folding laundry or consoling the kids when they are upset. Although hassles are not uncommon, Alex and Rachel have a close sibling relationship and regularly engage with new projects and activities.

The Sanchezes have many strengths and resources, but they also face significant challenges. Hannah's unplanned addition to the family is a source of stress due to her need for support with self-care and supervision to ensure her safety. She also makes frequent comments about the perceived dangers presented by certain toys or features of their old home (e.g., stairs, wood stove). Alex struggles with routine changes to and has periodic meltdowns when he cannot communicate effectively or has difficulty at school or during ABA sessions. Rachel also cries frequently, mostly when separated from Catherine. Beyond short fuses and meltdowns, the family's primary challenge relates to time; there are not always enough hours in the day to accomplish everything that needs to happen in their work and personal lives. Sleep is often compromised, with the children and Hannah waking up frequently. All four bedrooms are very close to one another, which causes concerns related to noise, and there is only one bathroom in their home, which creates an array of scheduling challenges. Figure 10.1 shows a summary of the family's strengths and challenges.

Catherine and Roberto felt they worked together to manage their busy lives well until Hannah moved in with them, shifting their family dynamics and changing many of their routines. Catherine and Roberto rarely had time together before engaging in the PBS process. They had lost the romantic spark, and their interactions tended to focus only on tasks or Hannah and their kids. The entire family was prone to frustration and had short fuses, with members frequently snapping at or avoiding each other. When the behavior analyst suggested Catherine and Roberto start a reinforcement system for Alex that would involve delivering tokens every 15 minutes for specific behaviors they

Sanchez Family	
Members: Roberto, Catherine, Alex, Rachel, and Grandma Hannah	
Strengths	**Challenges**
• Strong and supportive relationships	• Not enough time in the day
• Enjoyable jobs and all financial needs met	• Compromised and interrupted sleep
• Shared priority to take care of family members	• Short fuses and meltdowns
• Systems savvy, creating access to services	• Challenge with sharing and snatching/grabbing toys
• Support of responsive applied behavior analysis service providers	• Need for lots of supervision
• All family members share curiosity/love of learning	• Less romance/couple time

Figure 10.1.   The Sanchez family's Strengths and Challenges worksheet.

were addressing during their sessions, both parents balked because they were so overwhelmed with what they were already doing. The behavior analyst understood their concerns and explained that ABA could be applied in a much broader sense. The behavior analyst introduced Catherine and Roberto to the family-based PBS process in this book, explaining that the principles could be beneficial for their whole family. The Sanchezes wanted to regain the playful humor and positive energy that once characterized their family interactions and, therefore, committed to working through the PBS process with the behavior analyst's guidance and support.

STATUS BEFORE BEGINNING PROCESS

Catherine and Roberto began the process by working together to complete the Weekly Family Behavior Rating Tool one evening after the rest of the family was asleep (see Figure 10.2). They chose to complete the ratings on their own because Hannah and the children had limited understanding, patience, and reflection skills due to age or disability. Both parents agreed that completing chores thoroughly and correctly was a strength for their family, but they also saw that the parents took on the lion's share of the responsibility and it was not always clear who was responsible for different tasks. After much discussion, they ended up agreeing that their family "sometimes" engaged in all of the other behaviors listed on the rating form. They found that completing the rating led to extensive discussions about what was happening in the household and that it took sharing examples and negotiation to come to this consensus.

Catherine and Roberto identified "family members listen and respond to instructions without delay or argument" as their area of most significant challenge, and they also noted that speaking nicely and using gentle hands was not occurring as regularly as they hoped. They noted they frequently had to remind their children and Hannah to be gentle and respectful. They realized that Hannah's frequent comments about safety (e.g., be careful, watch out) and grabbing items she felt could be dangerous might have rubbed off on the children. Needing to share toys was a trigger for both children's meltdowns, and grabbing toys from one another was common. Rachel was more "rough and tumble" than Alex and would sometimes bite or hit him when things were not going her way.

After completing the weekly ratings, Catherine and Roberto decided to use the Family Interaction Journal to record specific successful and challenging times during one weekend (see Figure 10.3). They found that activities with clear expectations and roles for each family member seemed to be the most successful, whereas transitions with a time crunch were challenging and stressful.

Catherine and Roberto also worked together to complete the Family PBS Self-Check, reflecting on all family members' actions in their responses (see Figure 10.4). They agreed on most items but had longer and more complex

Weekly Family Behavior Rating				
	Never	Sometimes	Usually	Always
Family members complete their assigned chores (and homework) completely and correctly.	0	1	(2)	3
Family members listen and respond to instructions without delay or argument.	0	(1)	2	3
Family members respect one another's personal space and belongings.	0	(1)	2	3
Family members speak nicely and calmly with one another (e.g., no insults, name calling).	0	(1)	2	3
Family members use gentle hands when interacting (i e , no physical aggression).	0	(1)	2	3
Family members respect time lines, curfews, and other established limits.	0	(1)	2	3
Other (personal behavioral goals for your family) *A feeling of positive climate in the household (more positive than negative communication)*	0	(1)	2	3

Figure 10.2. The Sanchez family's Weekly Family Behavior Rating Tool.

conversations about the first section (Family Vision and Expectations) than any other section. They asked Alex if he knew the rules in their house, and he said "play nice" and "safe hands"; Catherine and Roberto were surprised by his response because although they often said these words to both kids, they had never clearly defined household expectations. The Sanchezes identified organization of time and space as an area of strength. They had a visual schedule in their kitchen and a shared electronic calendar, and both liked to keep their space organized with everything having a designated place. They discussed that some schedule changes were outside of their control (e.g., when the ABA service providers periodically needed to reschedule or cancel services due to

Family Interaction Journal		
At Our Best: Successful or Enjoyable Activity		
What was happening before and around us (e.g., activity)?	What did we each say or do?	How did everyone react, and what was the result?
Everyone had finished dinner and was preparing for bed. Roberto was with Rachel and Alex, Catherine was cleaning the kitchen, and Hannah was in the living room (occurs from 6:45 to 7:45 p.m. every night).	Roberto bathed Alex and Rachel together and used a timer for 10 minutes of washing followed by 10 minutes of play. Catherine cleaned the kitchen, put away the leftovers, and washed the dishes. Hannah talked to Catherine's sister on Skype in the living room, within earshot of Catherine.	Roberto and Catherine were able to accomplish their tasks quickly and with no hassles. The children and Hannah participated in activities that they enjoyed.
At Our Worst: Challenging or Frustrating Activity		
What was happening before and around us (e.g., activity)?	What did we each say or do?	How did everyone react, and what was the result?
Catherine and Hannah were rushing to leave on time for a Friday afternoon doctor's appointment for Hannah. Alex was working with his behavior technician in the living room during this transition. Roberto had just returned from work and was tired.	Hannah forgot things she needed, making it so Catherine and Hannah had to cut through the living room multiple times. Alex got upset they were leaving and became resistant with instructions. Roberto entered the scene to distract Alex, at which point Rachel started playing with the instructional materials and not following directions from Roberto or the ABA technician.	No one was doing what they were supposed to be doing. Catherine and Hannah were late for the appointment, Alex's ABA session was disrupted, and he became irritated with Rachel for playing with his materials. Tensions were high. Catherine scolded Hannah due to her frustration, and Roberto raised his voice with both children when they were not listening to him.

Figure 10.3.   The Sanchez family's Family Interaction Journal.

Family PBS Self-Check

Family name: *Sanchez*

Member(s) responding: *Catherine and Roberto*   Date: *9/1*

Please rate the degree that each the following are in place by checking the appropriate column.

Family Vision and Expectations	Not at all	Somewhat	Very much	Notes
Shared values and goals		X		*Mostly on the same page, but expectations and rules are not always clear or understood by all.*
Clear behavioral expectations		X		
Rules regarding misbehavior		X		
Household responsibilities		X		

Organization of Space and Time	Not at all	Somewhat	Very much	Notes
Good household organization			X	*A family strength. Some scheduling is outside of their control.*
Shared family calendar			X	
Consistent daily routines			X	
Notice of schedule changes		X		
Time limits on activities			X	

Teaching and Basic Discipline	Not at all	Somewhat	Very much	Notes
Explaining and modeling			X	*Primary focus on Alex's applied behavior analysis. A work in progress.*
Praise for positive behavior		X		
Privileges linked to behavior		X		
Pre-planned consequences		X		
Respectful discipline methods			X	

Supporting Family Life	Not at all	Somewhat	Very much	Notes
Open, clear communication			X	*Stress management is a key area of need. Community participation is challenging due to preference for two adults and conflicting schedules.*
General respect and kindness		X		
Effective problem resolution		X		
Strong, loving relationships			X	
Ability to manage stress	X			
Support of family and friends		X		
Full community participation		X		

Figure 10.4. The Sanchez family's Family PBS Self-Check.

staffing issues). Abrupt schedule changes set the stage for a shift in routines for all family members. Catherine and Roberto were pleased that the self-check captured their strengths (i.e., open communication, loving relationships) as well as challenges.

They identified stress management as their greatest challenge, noting that stress often resulted in additional disruption and hassles among family members. Catherine and Roberto rated all other elements of PBS in the middle. They recognized it would help to clarify their expectations, focus on encouraging desired behavior by all family members, and consider what adjustments and supports would help in every area.

Walking through this checklist left Catherine and Roberto feeling like they had a clear next step—they needed to work together to get everyone on the same page about values, goals, expectations, and responsibilities in their household. They believed this foundation would help everything run more smoothly.

■ WHAT DO YOU THINK? ■

Given this family's strengths and challenges, what supports do you think they need to improve their family functioning?

_____

_____

_____

_____

_____

_____

FAMILY VISION AND EXPECTATIONS

Next, the Sanchezes got to work on clarifying their family vision and expectations. Catherine and Roberto thought it would help to include Hannah in this step because she had always had valuable perspectives regarding family and shared past experiences, even though she could not consistently connect to current events. All three of the adults independently completed the exercise of circling specific values that were important to them. Then they compared notes over coffee while the kids ate breakfast on a Sunday morning. Catherine read the words aloud as she circled to help Hannah focus on the task. They all identified patience, togetherness, and perseverance as key values. Helpfulness and responsibility also were important to both Catherine and Roberto, and they agreed that these terms included everyone pitching in and helping each other without being asked. They felt that these traits contributed to an overall positive climate among all family members in their household. They used their conversations about these key values to develop this vision statement: *The Sanchez family is understanding, patient, and helpful toward all family members to remain positive when things are good* and *challenging.*

■ WHAT DO YOU THINK? ■

Given the vision and priorities of this family, what behavioral expectations do you think would be important for them?

_____

_____

_____

_____

_____

_____

Catherine and Roberto then used their identified values and mission to define their expectations and rules. They first thought about expectations adopted by the ABA service team and in other settings such as Alex's preschool classroom, considering how to connect those goals with their family vision and expectations. Alex's ABA providers had three main expectations: listen the first time, try your best, and respect the materials. These did not seem particularly relevant to the family because their primary focus was keeping Alex engaged in their instructional program. The expectations at Alex's preschool were to Practice Kindness, Act Responsibly, Work Together (PAW). These expectations were in close alignment with the family's vision, emphasizing patience, understanding, and working together. Catherine and Roberto decided to adopt these three simple expectations for their family, given how young their children were and how well Alex seemed to understand his school's and ABA session expectations.

To clarify the behaviors associated with each of the PAW expectations, Catherine and Roberto developed a chart with examples and nonexamples of each expectation (see Figure 10.5). This level of clarification was important given the complex challenges faced by their family. This chart specified which behaviors would likely result in positive consequences and those that would contradict the expectations. To consistently employ these expectations, Catherine and Roberto recognized that everyone in the family would need to think about others' feelings and perspectives, sometimes making sacrifices for the betterment of the family and learning to manage their stress (i.e., see the Teaching Behavioral Expectations section for examples of calming down practices).

Expectation	Examples	Nonexamples
Practice Kindness	• Listening actively to one another (e.g., eye contact, questioning) • Communicating feelings and needs appropriately • Asking permission to use others' belongings before touching or taking them • Using gentle hands	• Looking or walking away, placating (e.g., "uh huh") • Yelling, screaming, criticizing, and blaming • Grabbing or taking items without permission • Pushing, hitting
Act Responsibly	• Following instructions the first time they are presented • Adhering to commitments • Taking care of belongings and using items as intended • Completing assigned chores	• Ignoring, walking away, making excuses, or delaying tasks • Slamming, breaking, or otherwise misusing items • Failing to complete responsibilities in time frames provided
Work Together	• Asking for help or space when needed • Offering assistance when help appears needed • Resolving problems together	• Complaining, "suffering in silence," or having meltdowns • Ignoring the needs of others • Creating quick fixes or leaving problems to fester

Figure 10.5. Examples and nonexamples for family expectations.

Developing the PAW expectations also led to the development of rules and time lines. The Sanchez family struggled to respect personal space and belongings, respond to changes in routines, and problem-solve when things went awry. Therefore, they adopted the following rules.

1. Before taking anyone's belongings or entering their rooms, you must have permission. If an argument erupts over an item, then an adult will remove the item until a resolution can be reached regarding who will have it.

2. Any time the schedule needs to be changed, the person making the change will immediately notify everyone affected and update the shared calendar.

Appointments or plans not included in the calendar may need to be canceled or modified.

3. If you have a specific concern, then bring it to a parent rather than taking things into your own hands. They will help you resolve the problem.

Time lines that were important to the family included use of the bathroom and Catherine's office time. The family agreed that they would each have no more than 15 minutes in the bathroom each morning, with their times scheduled based on when they needed to leave the house. They also clarified that Catherine was not to be disturbed during work hours unless an emergency would affect someone's safety and Roberto was unavailable.

◼ WHAT DO YOU THINK? ◼

Given the background information on this family, what changes might be helpful in their household, schedule, and routines?

_____

_____

_____

_____

_____

_____

ARRANGING SPACE AND TIME

Although Catherine and Roberto identified organization of space and time as a strength on the self-check, they welcomed the opportunity to think through how to make their space work better. In doing this, they first considered areas or aspects of their home that seemed to be associated with challenges. Catherine quickly identified her office space, which extended from the living room, as problematic. Hannah and the kids often approached Catherine while working, and the behavior technicians also interrupted her work flow with loud praise or requests for materials (e.g., scissors, paper). Roberto identified his greatest frustration as finding everything they needed to get out the door on time, especially in the winter when they required more gear (e.g., boots, hats, mittens, snow pants).

They purchased and installed French doors to provide more physical separation between the living and office spaces. They then installed sticker panels on the glass to obstruct the kids' vision of their mother because Rachel began to stand and try to get Catherine's attention through the glass panels. Catherine also purchased a stop/go sign for the door knob to serve as a visual indicator of whether any family member or behavior technician could enter her office and interrupt her work. Together, Catherine and Roberto came up with an arrangement for their kitchen, which is where they entered and exited the house. They organized the space with hooks, cubbies, and pictures of what the areas looked like when things were in their correct places to increase Hannah's, Alex's, and Rachel's independence when they were leaving the house or returning from an outing.

One of Hannah's primary challenges was that she often would have trouble finding her room, often multiple times each day. So, they decided to create self-portraits together as a family to frame and clearly display on each bedroom door to help Hannah increase her independence with locating the correct upstairs bedroom. They also decided to leave a few snacks and water bottles in Hannah's room because she would also often interrupt other family routines to request a snack or drink. She would also get disoriented and not find her way back to her room after going downstairs to the refrigerator.

Catherine and Roberto then thought about their daily schedule and times that were most challenging or most likely to contribute to frustration. The couple agreed that the routine of bath time and bedtime after dinner, which was once an example of effective division and conquering of tasks, was no longer working. This time was more challenging with Hannah living with them because she also needed supervision. She often wanted help finding her room or getting ready for bed while Catherine was trying to clean up after the meal and Roberto was bathing the children. Catherine enlisted her sister, who used to be Hannah's primary caregiver before experiencing her own mental health challenges, to talk to their mother on Skype every night during this window of time to keep Hannah occupied during the regular bath time and kitchen clean-up routine. This change in routine served multiple purposes. Not only did it keep Hannah busy as she enjoyed the daily visits with her daughter, but it also reduced the calls and texts from Catherine's sister each day requesting to talk to Hannah at times that were inconvenient for Catherine.

The Sanchezes already used a shared electronic calendar for family activities and appointments. Catherine and Roberto also had systems to communicate throughout the day and had no concerns about their use of their time. Although some people could see their 20 hours a week of home-based ABA treatment as a burden, they recognized that they had learned to go about their daily lives with the service providers there. They noted that the structured schedule for ABA services, which did sometimes change unexpectedly, helped the family stick to a tight schedule and routine throughout their weekdays. Given the difficulties during transitions, the Sanchezes determined that having behavior technicians working with Alex at these times was a benefit. They worked collaboratively with their ABA treatment team and prioritized transitions times for ABA services while ensuring that dinner and bath time was protected family time (i.e., ABA providers were not welcome during these daily routines).

◼ WHAT DO YOU THINK? ◼

How might the skills this family felt needed to be developed be taught
and reinforced? How might you deal with behavior that violates family
expectations?

_____

_____

_____

_____

_____

_____

TEACHING BEHAVIORAL EXPECTATIONS

While clarifying their expectations and evaluating their family routines, the
Sanchezes identified two skill areas on which all family members needed to
work—self-management and daily living/personal care. These skills related
directly to the family's PAW expectations and the family vision of being positive and supportive. Self-management was an area targeted for improvement
among all five family members. The specific skills, which the family referred
to as _calm down practices_, included counting to three before responding,
taking five deep breaths to relax, and requesting space from other family
members (self–time-out). They also focused on teaching perspective-taking
strategies to the children and Hannah to help them demonstrate empathy for
others. They would remind each other to "put yourself in their shoes" or use
an emotion identification chart and guess how a person may be feeling. With
guidance from the behavior analyst, each of these self-management skills was
pretaught during relaxed down time. Family members were then prompted
with words such as _breathe_ or with the emotion chart (or both) to use the
strategies in times of high frustration. The emotion chart became part of daily
breakfast conversations, and the family made a game of mimicking the faces
on the chart and having other family members guess the emotion. Catherine
and Roberto agreed to immediately honor all requests for space from any family member to reward their efforts to use appropriate strategies. The family
worked on deep breathing before and after every meal as an opportunity to
practice this skill within daily routines. In addition, Catherine and Roberto
both agreed to ask each other for help when they felt their fuses were short and
needed a break.

Sharing and asking permission to use toys or touch other belongings was
another aspect of self-management important in the Sanchez family. Because
Roberto was home more, he took the lead in prompting Alex and Rachel to say,
"May I have _____?" and wait for a response before taking items as well as give
up items in their possession when asked nicely. Catherine and Roberto looked

for natural opportunities to praise sharing and asking permission among all family members throughout the day.

Independence with daily living tasks was a primary concern for Hannah and the two children, with transitions in and out of the house and after dinner/ before bedtime identified as the most chaotic times for all family members and when independence was least likely. All family members learned how to appropriately use their "touch down space" in the reorganized kitchen to get everything they needed (e.g., coats, bags, shoes) to leave the house. The parents modeled getting their items together while they talked aloud (e.g., "Let's see, I need ____ and ____. I'll put those in my bag"). Once Hannah and the children got the hang of the transitions, they were encouraged to rely on the visual reminders (pictures in the kitchen of what the space should look like when everything has its place). The parents and behavioral services team used explicit repeated instruction with visual supports to teach Alex to zip his jacket and put on his boots by himself and teach both Alex and Rachel how to clear their plates from the table after dinner. They gave the children and Hannah feedback, praise, and rewards for any time they demonstrated a new skill. Catherine also asked Hannah to fold laundry for the whole family, a task she was able to perform with minimal support (i.e., someone else had to bring the laundry basket up from the basement) once they demonstrated the task for her just a few times as folding laundry was a skill she already had. When Hannah was assigned to fold the laundry, it removed a large chore off of Roberto's and Catherine's plates and helped Hannah stay busy during chaotic times. Hannah also felt good that she was contributing to the household. Last, Roberto taught Alex how to feed the Venus flytrap and water the other house plants. Managing these responsibilities became a special morning routine shared by Roberto and Alex. Listing and assigning all household tasks was an important step for Roberto and Catherine since they were balancing many responsibilities related to daily living (see Figure 10.6).

The Sanchezes made a game out of their transitions out of the house to keep in line with their mission to encourage the family to help and support one another during challenging times. They timed how long it took them to get out of the house for each weekend outing and tried to beat the clock from last weekend's time. If they beat the clock, then they listened to special music in the car instead of the radio; if all family members practiced kindness toward one another, then the kids could watch their tablet in the car that day.

As previously mentioned, when Alex's behavior analyst initially suggested using a token-based reinforcement system for him, Catherine and Roberto hesitated, given the other demands on their time. Once the family PBS structures were in place and their stress had decreased, they felt it would be more doable, especially if it could be used with Rachel as well. They decided to adopt the same sticker chart that existed for Alex as part of his school–home and ABA program, except they used the PAW expectations. They reviewed the PAW expectations with the children every evening after bath time and provided stickers for meeting the expectations and praised their successes. They

Household tasks	Family member(s) responsible
Grocery shopping	Roberto
Meal planning	Catherine
Cooking	Roberto (weekdays); Catherine (weekends)
Doing dishes	Roberto (daytime); Catherine (nighttime)
Cleaning up toys	Alex and Rachel
Bathing	Roberto (Alex and Rachel); Catherine (Hannah)
Tidying	Catherine
Deep cleaning	Catherine
Trash and recycling	Roberto
Yard work/snow removal	Roberto
Laundry	Catherine (doing laundry); Hannah (folding laundry)
Taking care of the dog	Roberto
Taking care of the cat	Catherine
Taking care of the plants	Alex
Coordinating services and medical appointments	Catherine
Coordinating automotive and home maintenance appointments	Roberto

Figure 10.6. The Sanchez family's household task assignments.

also added individual goals for each child, including Rachel separating from Catherine and Alex handling transitions and other changes without meltdowns. Each week, they set goals for how many stickers the children could earn. If the children met the goal, then they got to pick one special activity in which all family members would participate. In addition, they capitalized on natural reinforcement opportunities to encourage more positive transitions by developing a schedule that arranged for less preferred activities before (rather than after) more preferred activities (e.g., wash time happens before playtime during the bath routine).

Catherine and Roberto got in the habit of praising one another when they were proactive and positive. They also gently reminded each other when they slipped. They developed a system to "tap" each other in and out during stressful situations, which helped them maintain composure and feel supported by one another. Finally, the parents also decided to reward themselves when they consistently followed their PAW expectations. They each would get time alone on weekends (i.e., solo grocery store trips for Roberto, coffee dates with a friend for Catherine).

■ WHAT DO YOU THINK? ■

Given what you have learned about this family, how might they monitor their interactions and address challenges as they arise?

_____

_____

_____

_____

_____

_____

MONITORING OUTCOMES AND PROBLEM SOLVING

Catherine and Roberto served as models and coaches for each other and provided frequent support, praise, and feedback in the moment to the children and Hannah. During their nightly chats after Hannah and the children were in bed, they reviewed their family plan and reflected on what was going well and areas they felt they could improve. Both parents realized that being more intentional in using encouraging words and managing their frustration levels, redistributing the household tasks, and scheduling time for themselves each week had changed the dynamics among all members of their household and improved their daily quality of life.

The Sanchez family completed the Family PBS Self-Check (see Figure 10.7) again 6 months after they were introduced to the PBS process by their ABA providers. The family had a lot to celebrate, including all members articulating their family values and expectations, having more kind and respectful interactions, and developing new skills that increased the distribution of responsibility and independence of all family members as well as reducing stress. Overall, they felt that their scheduling and household organization continued to stabilize, and transitions had become smoother. The parents were also proud of their improvement in effective teaching practices, including modeling and rewarding desired behavior.

Family PBS Self-Check

Family name: *Sanchez*

Member(s) responding: *Catherine and Roberto*   Date: *3/1*

Please rate the degree that each the following are in place by checking the appropriate column.

Family Vision and Expectations	Not at all	Somewhat	Very much
Shared values and goals			X
Clear behavioral expectations			X
Rules regarding misbehavior			X
Household responsibilities			X
Organization of Space and Time	**Not at all**	**Somewhat**	**Very much**
Good household organization			X
Shared family calendar			X
Consistent daily routines			X
Notice of schedule changes		X	
Time limits on activities			X
Teaching and Basic Discipline	**Not at all**	**Somewhat**	**Very much**
Explaining and modeling			X
Praise for positive behavior			X
Privileges linked to behavior		X	
Pre-planned consequences		X	
Respectful discipline methods			X
Supporting Family Life	**Not at all**	**Somewhat**	**Very much**
Open, clear communication			X
General respect and kindness			X
Effective problem resolution		X	
Strong, loving relationships			X
Ability to manage stress		X	
Support of family and friends		X	
Full community participation			X

Figure 10.7. The Sanchez family's Family PBS Self-Check, 6 months after starting their plan.

Their assessment also helped to identify parts of their plan that needed to be enhanced. The family routines had been disrupted by recent schedule changes associated with work, school, and ABA services, and the parents were sometimes delayed in notifying one another and noting the changes on the calendar. The parents agreed to text one another right away going forward. Because Alex's behavioral services team were a big part of their daily lives, the Sanchezes worked closely with them to ensure that sessions were scheduled at the right times and did not interfere with valued family routines. Challenges continued around everyone sharing one bathroom. They decided that all activities that did not involve water (e.g., brushing/drying hair, applying makeup, dressing) would be done in their rooms to keep the bathroom free from unnecessary traffic and began budgeting for construction on an additional bathroom.

They noted that providing privileges and consequences were still challenging because the children were so young and Hannah relied so heavily on support from Catherine and Roberto. The parents decided to reward the entire family with a special outing each week when everyone completed their assigned chores. The parents also agreed to limit electronic devices to days when the children met the expectations on the sticker chart.

MAKING IT WORK

The Sanchezes were skilled in negotiating conflicts in their busy schedules, which speaks to their open communication and willingness to be flexible with their work schedules and personal needs of all family members. Their breakdowns in communication seemed to relate to time and access to one another, rather than a reflection on their willingness to connect. Catherine and Roberto worked well together, but the strain on their marriage because of their demanding lives was apparent. They decided to carve out a weekly date night. A baby sitter would come after the kids and Hannah went to bed, allowing them to go out for dinner to reconnect with one another as a couple. They initially decided not to go out earlier for fear that things would go awry with Hannah and the kids. Over time, with help from Alex's behavioral service team and the baby sitter, the children and Hannah increased their independence, making it possible for Catherine and Roberto to leave while everyone was still awake so they could include friends. Catherine and Roberto agreed to avoid discussing family issues during their dates to focus on each other, thereby strengthening their relationship.

Throughout the PBS process, the Sanchezes learned the importance of stress management for all family members and spending quality family time together. They decided to do guided yoga as a family at least once a week using videos from YouTube. This activity allowed for some fun yet structured family time to work toward their self-management goal and overall stress reduction together. Weekend outings, which were also part of Alex's weekly ABA goals to promote his community engagement, were also targeted as a time for family fun. Alex's behavior analyst provided consultation related to outings but did not attend with the family. The family selected activities and locations, planned the outings together, read material about the outings, and got everyone involved. The Sanchezes made sure to choose outings that Hannah could also attend and enjoy (e.g., aquarium, zoo, park). They even purchased a larger vehicle to make these trips possible with two car seats, three adults, and sometimes a dog.

The Sanchezes realized they had isolated themselves and were not fully using outside support available to them. They decided that getting a housekeeper to come every other week for a major cleaning would be worth the cost. Thanks to the parents' systems savviness, they were able to gain access to respite care for both Alex and Hannah through state disability services. Hannah started attending a supervised crafts class at the community center for 2 hours twice per week. She also had a home health aide come to the house to assist her with bathing and other self-care twice per week, reducing the demands on Catherine. Alex was allotted 4 hours of respite, during which time the parents could spend more one-to-one time with Rachel or enjoy extended rendezvous as a couple. The Sanchez family realized they tended to focus heavily on Alex's treatments and Hannah's care, and this provided a way to balance their attention.

Catherine and Roberto found the need for self-reflection as they worked through the PBS process. Catherine learned that, outside her career, she had come to identify herself personally as only a caregiver. She had difficulty giving up control and delegating responsibility, worrying that others would forget something or do it wrong, which created a feeling of hypervigilance that was not healthy for her or others. Roberto learned that he tended to disconnect and just go through the motions when things got challenging. In doing so, he often did forget details. The couple recognized that caregiving was an essential part of their lives, but it shouldn't define them. They identified an online support group for caregivers and began posting and responding to get perspectives of others in their shoes and to vent when needed. This group, and all of the other PBS supports, resulted in a significant improvement in the Sanchezes' lives, and they committed to continue monitoring and problem solving using this framework going forward.

SUMMARY: HELPING YOUR FAMILY
THRIVE WITH POSITIVE BEHAVIOR SUPPORT

PBS is a proactive and educative approach for promoting desired behavior. It has been used extensively within schools and organizations to improve the behavior of children and adults. Although PBS has been applied extensively to address the behavior of individual children within families, there is a gap in the literature regarding implementation for entire families. In this book, we guided you through a process of assessment, plan design, and implementation to clarify expectations, structure space and time, teach and reward desired behavior (while effectively responding to misbehavior), and monitor outcomes for your entire family. We hope that the process and strategies you developed will benefit all members of your family and can be used for ongoing planning and problem solving.

Resources

WEB SITES

Home and Community Positive Behavior Support Network: Families Page: https://hcpbs.org/families-3

Association for Positive Behavior Support: Families Page: https://www.apbs.org/pbs/gettingstarted/getting-started-with-pbis-families

National Center for Pyramid Model Innovation: http://challengingbehavior.cbcs.usf.edu

Center for Parent Information and Resources: https://www.parentcenterhub.org

OSEP Technical Assistance Center on Positive Behavior Interventions and Support: http://www.pbis.org

VIDEOS

Positive Behavior Support Special Issue, Parenting Special Needs Magazine: https://magazine.parentingspecialneeds.org/publication/?i=461820

Practiced Routines PBS Parent Training Videos: https://www.youtube.com/playlist?list=PLLi08Aejqezrdyq4rTcBUmI63EzBKPNkx

Positive Solutions Parent Training Modules (CSEFEL): http://csefel.vanderbilt.edu/resources/training_parent.html

BOOKS: POSITIVE BEHAVIOR SUPPORT

Carr, E. G., Levin, L., McConnachie, G., Carlson, J. I., Kemp, D. C., & Smith, C. E. (1994). *Communication-based intervention for problem behavior: A user's guide for producing positive change.* Paul H. Brookes Publishing Co.

Dishion, T. J., & Stormshak, E. A. (2007). *Intervening in children's lives: An ecological, family-centered approach to mental health care.* American Psychological Association.

Dunlap, G., Strain, P. S., Lee, J. K., Joseph, J., Vatland, C., & Fox, L. S. (2017). *Prevent-teach-reinforce for families: A model of individualized positive behavior support for home and community.* Paul H. Brookes Publishing Co.

Durand, V. M. (2011). *Optimistic parenting: Hope and help for you and your challenging child.* Paul H. Brookes Publishing Co.

Hieneman, M., Elfner, K., & Sergay, J. (2022). *Resolving your child's challenging behavior: A practical guide to parenting with positive behavior support.* Paul H. Brookes Publishing Co.

Lucyshyn, J. M., Dunlap, G., & Albin, R. W. (2002). *Families and positive behavior support: Addressing problem behavior in family contexts.* Paul H. Brookes Publishing Co.

O'Neill, R. E., Albin, R. W., Storey, K., Horner, R. H., & Sprague, J. R. (2015). *Functional and program development for problem behavior: A practical handbook.* Cengage Learning.

BOOKS: PARENTING

Brazelton, T. B. & Sparrow, J. (2015). *Discipline: The Brazelton way*. Da Capo Press.

Brooks, H. (2020). *Practical positive parenting: How to raise emotionally-intelligent children ages 2–7 by empowering confidence*. Practical Positive Parenting.

Delahooke, M. (2019). *Beyond behaviors: Using brain science to understand and solve children's behavioral challenges*. PESI.

Faber, A., & Mazlish, E. (2012). *How to talk so kids will listen and listen so kids will talk*. Scribner.

Gordon, T. (2008). *Parent effectiveness training: The proven program for raising responsible children*. Three Rivers Press.

Greene, R. W. (2021). *The explosive child: A new approach for understanding and parenting frustrated, chronically inflexible children* (4th ed.). Harper.

Kabat-Zinn, M., & Kabat-Zinn, J. (2014). *Everyday blessings: The inner work of mindful parenting* (Rev. ed.). Hachette.

Nelsen, J. (2006). *Positive discipline: The classic guide to helping children develop self-discipline, responsibility, cooperation, and problem-solving skills*. Random House.

Phifer, L., Sibbald, L., & Roden, J. (2018). *Parenting toolbox: 125 activities therapists use to reduce meltdowns, increase positive behaviors, and manage motions*. PESI Parenting.

Race, K. (2014). *Mindful parenting: Simple and powerful solutions for raising creative, engaged, happy kids in today's hectic world*. St. Martin's Griffin.

Siegel, D. J., & Bryson, T. P. (2014). *No-drama discipline: The whole brain way to calm the chaos and nurture your child's developing mind*. Bantam.

Siegel, D. J., & Hartzell, M. (2013). *Parenting from the inside out: How a deeper understanding can help you raise children who thrive*. Penguin.

Tsabary, S. (2010). *The conscious parent: Transforming ourselves, empowering our children*. Namaste Publishing.

BOOKS: POSITIVE PSYCHOLOGY

Seligman, M. E. P. (2006). *Learned optimism: How to change your mind and your life*. Random House. (Originally published in 1991 by Alfred A. Knopf.)

Bibliography

POSITIVE BEHAVIOR SUPPORT FOR FAMILIES

Cheremshynski, C., Lucyshyn, J. M., & Olson, D. L. (2013). Implementation of a culturally appropriate positive behavior support plan with a Japanese mother of a child with autism: An experimental and qualitative analysis. *Journal of Positive Behavior Interventions, 15*(4), 242–253.

Duda, M. A., Dunlap, G., Fox, L., Lentini, R., & Clarke, S. (2004). An experimental evaluation of positive behavior support in a community preschool program. *Topics in Early Childhood Special Education, 24*(3), 143–155.

Dunlap, G., Carr, E. G., Horner, R. H., Koegel, R. L., Sailor, W., Clarke, S., Koegel, L. K., Albin, R. W., Vaughn, B. J., McLaughlin, D. M., James, K. M., Todd, A. W., Newton, J. S., Lucyshyn, J., Griggs, P., Bohanon, H., Choi, J. H., Vismara, L., Minjarez, M. B., Buschbacher, P., & Fox, L. (2010). A descriptive, multiyear examination of positive behavior support. *Behavioral Disorders, 35*(4), 259–279.

Durand, V. M., Hieneman, M., Clarke, S., Wang, M., & Rinaldi, M. L. (2012). Positive family intervention for severe challenging behavior I: A multisite randomized clinical trial. *Journal of Positive Behavior Interventions, 15*(3), 133–143.

Hieneman, M., Elfner, K., & Sergay, J. (2022). *Resolving your child's challenging behavior: A practical guide to parenting with positive behavior support.* Paul H. Brookes Publishing Co.

Hieneman, M., & Fefer, S. A. (2017). Employing the principles of positive behavior support to enhance family education and intervention. *Journal of Child and Family Studies, 26*(10), 2655–2668.

Lucyshyn, J., Binnendyk, L., Fossett, B., Cheremshynski, S., Lohrmann, S., Elkinson, L., & Miller, L. (2009). Toward an ecological unit of analysis in behavioral assessment and intervention with families of children with developmental disabilities. In W. Sailor, G. Dunlap, G. Sugai, & R. Horner (Eds.), *Handbook of positive behavior support* (pp. 73–106). Springer.

Lucyshyn, J. M., Albin, R. W., Horner, R. H., Mann, J. C., Mann, J. A., & Wadsworth, G. (2007). Family implementation of positive behavior support for a child with autism: Longitudinal, single-case, experimental, and descriptive replication and extension. *Journal of Positive Behavior Interventions, 9*(3), 131–150. doi:10.1177/10983007070090030201

Lucyshyn, J. M., Dunlap, G., & Albin, R. W. (2002). *Families and positive behavior support: Addressing problem behavior in family contexts.* Paul H. Brookes Publishing Co.

COPARENTING AND RESPONSIBILITY

Baril, M. E., Crouter, A. C., & McHale, S. M. (2007). Processes linking adolescent well-being, marital love, and coparenting. *Journal of Family Psychology, 21*(4), 645.

Feinberg, M. E., & Kan, M. L. (2008). Establishing family foundations: Intervention effects on coparenting, parent/infant well-being, and parent-child relations. *Journal of Family Psychology, 22*(2), 253.

Feinberg, M. E., Kan, M. L., & Hetherington, E. M. (2007). The longitudinal influence of coparenting conflict on parental negativity and adolescent maladjustment. *Journal of Marriage and Family, 69*(3), 687–702.

McHale, J. P. (Ed.). (2011). Coparenting in diverse family systems. In J. P. McHale & K. M. Lindahl (Eds.), *Coparenting: A conceptual and clinical examination of family systems* (pp. 15–37). American Psychological Association.

Pew Research Center. (2015). *Parenting in America: Outlook, worries, aspirations, are strongly linked to financial situation.* Retrieved from https://www.pewresearch.org/social -trends/2015/12/17/parenting-in-america/

Riina, E. M., & McHale, S. M. (2014). Bidirectional influences between dimensions of coparenting and adolescent adjustment. *Journal of Youth and Adolescence, 43*(2), 257–269.

RULES AND RESPONSIBILITIES

Barton, A. W., Brody, G. H., Yu, T., Kogan, S. M., Chen, E., & Ehrlich, K. B. (2019). The profundity of the everyday: Family routines in adolescence predict development in young adulthood. *Journal of Adolescent Health, 64*(3), 340–346. https://doi-org.silk.library.umass.edu /10.1016/j.jadohealth.2018.08.029

Buschbacher, P., Fox, L., & Clarke, S. (2004). Recapturing desired family routines: A parent–professional behavioral collaboration. *Research and Practice for Persons with Severe Disabilities, 29*, 25–39.

Covey, S. R. (1997). *The 7 habits of highly effective families.* Golden Books.

Ferretti, L. K., & Bub, K. L. (2014). The influence of family routines on the resilience of low-income preschoolers. *Journal of Applied Developmental Psychology, 35*(3), 168–180. https://doi-org.silk.library.umass.edu/10.1016/j.appdev.2014.03.003

Gralinkski, H., & Kopp, C. (1993). Everyday rules for behavior: Mothers' requests to young children. *Developmental Psychology, 29*(3), 573–584.

Helton, J. J., Schreiber, J. C., Wiley, J., & Schweitzer, R. (2018). Finding a routine that works: A mixed methods study of foster parents. *Child and Family Social Work, 23*(2), 248–255. https://doi-org.silk.library.umass.edu/10.1111/cfs.12412

Hill, J., & Holmbeck, G. (1987). Disagreement about rules in families with seventh-grade girls and boys. *Journal of Youth and Adolescence, 16*(3), 221–246.

Lagattuta, K. H. (2005). When you shouldn't do what you want to do: Young children's understanding of desires, rules, and emotions. *Child Development, 76*(3), 713–733.

Larsen, K. L., & Jordan, S. S. (2020). Organized chaos: Daily routines link household chaos and child behavior problems. *Journal of Child and Family Studies, 29*, 1094–1107. https://doi .org/10.1007/s10826-019-01645-9

Phillips, T. M., Wilmoth, J. D., Wheeler, B. E., Turner, J. J., Shaw, E. E., & Brooks, C. (2018). Observance of regular family routines by family structure. *Journal of Family and Consumer Sciences, 110*(4), 22–26.

Wang, R., Bianchi, S., & Raley, S. (2005). Teenagers' Internet use and family rules: A research note. *Journal of Marriage and Family, 67*(5), 1249–1258.

ENVIRONMENTAL ARRANGEMENT

Blair, K. S. C., Lee, I. S., Cho, S. J., & Dunlap, G. (2011). Positive behavior support through family–school collaboration for young children with autism. *Topics in Early Childhood Special Education, 31*(1), 22–36.

Joseph, J. D., Strain, P. S., & Dunlap, G. (2021). An experimental analysis of Prevent Teach Reinforce for Families (PTR-F). *Topics in Early Childhood Special Education, 41*(2), 115–128.

Lucyshyn, J. M., Miller, L. D., Cheremshynski, C., Lohrmann, S., & Zumbo, B. D. (2018). Transforming coercive processes in family routines: Family functioning outcomes for families of children with developmental disabilities. *Journal of Child and Family Studies, 27*(9), 2844–2861.

Luiselli, J. K. (2006). *Antecedent assessment and intervention: Supporting children and adults with developmental disabilities in community settings.* Paul H. Brookes Publishing Co.

O'Neill, R. E., Hawken, L. S., & Bundock, K. (2015). Conducting functional behavioral assessments. In F. Brown, J. L. Anderson, & R. L. De Pry (Eds.), *Individual positive behavior supports: A standards-based guide to practices in school and community settings* (pp. 259–278). Paul H. Brookes Publishing Co.

Radley, K. C., & Dart, E. H. (2016). Antecedent strategies to promote children's and adolescents' compliance with adult requests: A review of the literature. *Clinical Child and Family Psychology Review, 19*(1), 39–54.

Stichter, J. P., Hudson, S., & Sasso, G. P. (2005). The use of structural analysis to identify setting events in applied settings for students with emotional/behavioral disorders. *Behavioral Disorders, 30*, 403–420. http://www.jstor.org/stable/23889852

AMERICAN ACADEMY OF PEDIATRICS POSITIVE DISCIPLINE

Knopf, A. (2019). AAP reaffirms: Spanking doesn't work and is harmful to mental health. *Brown University Child and Adolescent Behavior Letter, 34*(6), 9–10.

Sege, R. D., & Siegel, B. S., Council on Child Abuse and Neglect, Committee on Psychosocial Aspects of Child and Family Health, American Academy of Pediatrics. (2018). Effective discipline to raise healthy children. *Pediatrics, 142*, e20183112.

CONSEQUENCE-BASED STRATEGIES

Athens, E. S., & Vollmer, T. R. (2010). An investigation of differential reinforcement of alternative behaviors without extinction. *Journal of Applied Behavior Analysis, 43*, 569–589.

Clarke, S., Dunlap, G., & Vaughn, B. (1999). Family-centered, assessment-based intervention to improve behavior during an early morning routine. *Journal of Positive Behavior Interventions, 1*, 235–241.

Hanley, G. P., Iwata, B. A., & McCord, B. E. (2003). Functional analysis of problem behavior: A review. *Journal of Applied Behavior Analysis, 36*, 147–185.

Ingram, K., Lewis-Palmer, T., & Sugai, G. (2005). Function-based intervention planning: Comparing the effectiveness of FBA function-based and non-function-based intervention plans. *Journal of Positive Behavior Interventions, 7*, 224–236. doi:10.1177/10983007050070040401

Leijten, P., Gardner, F., Melendez-Torres, G. J., van Aar, J., Hutchings, J., Schulz, S., Knerr, W., & Overbeek, G. (2019). Meta-analyses: Key parenting program components for disruptive child behavior. *Journal of the American Academy of Child and Adolescent Psychiatry, 58*(2), 180–190.

Skinner, B. F. (1938). *The behavior of organisms: An experimental analysis.* Appleton-Century.

Wacker, D. P., Berg, W. K., Harding, J. W., & Cooper-Brown, L. J. (2011). Functional and structural approaches to behavioral assessment of problem behavior. In W. W. Fisher, C. C. Piazza, & H. S. Roane (Eds.), *Handbook of applied behavior analysis* (pp. 165–181). Guilford Press.

FAMILY INTERVENTION PROGRAMS

Dittman, C. K., Farruggia, S. P., Keown, L. J., & Sanders, M. R. (n.d.). Dealing with disobedience: An evaluation of a brief parenting intervention for young children showing noncompliant behavior problems. *Child Psychiatry and Human Development, 47*(1), 102–112.

Durand, V. M. (2011). *Optimistic parenting: Hope and help for you and your challenging child.* Paul H. Brookes Publishing Co.

The Gottman Institute. (n.d.). *A research-based approach to relationships.* Retrieved from https://www.gottman.com

Kabat-Zinn, M., & Kabat-Zinn, J. (2014). *Everyday blessings: The inner work of mindful parenting (Rev. ed.).* Hachette.

Race, K. (2014). *Mindful parenting: Simple and powerful solutions for raising creative, engaged, happy kids in today's hectic world.* St. Martin's Griffin.

Sanders, M. R. (1999). Triple P-Positive Parenting Program: Towards an empirically validated multilevel parenting and family support strategy for the prevention of behavior and emotional problems in children. *Clinical Child and Family Psychology Review, 2*(2), 71–91.

Sanders, M. R., & McFarland, M. (2000). Treatment of depressed mothers with disruptive children: A controlled evaluation of cognitive behavioral family intervention. *Behavior Therapy, 31*, 89–112. doi:10.1016/S0005-7894(00)80006-4

Sanders, M. R., Turner, K. M., & Markie-Dadds, C. (2002). The development and dissemination of the Triple P-Positive Parenting Program: A multilevel, evidence-based system of parenting and family support. *Prevention Science, 3*(3), 173–189. doi:10. 1023/A:1019942516231

Turner, K. M. T., & Sanders, M. R. (2006). Dissemination of evidence-based parenting and family support strategies: Learning from the Triple P-Positive Parenting Program system approach. *Aggression and Violent Behavior, 11*, 176–193. doi:10.1016/j. avb.2005.07.005

Webster-Stratton, C. (2005). The incredible years: A training series for the prevention and treatment of conduct problems in young children. In E. D. Hibbs & P. S. Jensen (Eds.), *Psychosocial treatments for child and adolescent disorders: Empirically based strategies for clinical practice* (pp. 507–555). American Psychological Association.

Webster-Stratton, C., & Hammond, M. (1997). Treating children with early-onset conduct problems: A comparison of child and parent training interventions. *Journal of Consulting and Clinical Psychology, 65*(1), 93. doi:10.1037/0022-006X.65.1.93

BEHAVIORAL SKILLS TRAINING

Baker, B. L., & Brightman, A. J. (2004). *Steps to independence: Teaching everyday skills to children with special needs* (4th ed.). Paul H. Brookes Publishing Co.

Drifke, M. A., Tiger, J. H., & Wierzba, B. C. (2017). Using behavioral skills training to teach parents to implement three-step prompting: A component analysis and generalization assessment. *Learning and Motivation, 57*, 1–14.

LaBrot, Z. C., Radley, K. C., Dart, E., Moore, J., & Cavell, H. J. (2018). A component analysis of behavioral skills training for effective instruction delivery. *Journal of Family Psychotherapy, 29*(2), 122–141.

Tiger, J. H., Hanley, G. P., & Bruzek, J. (2008). Functional communication training: A review and practical guide. *Behavior Analysis in Practice, 1*, 16–23. https://www.ncbi.nlm.nih.gov /pmc/articles/ PMC2846575

Ward-Horner, J., & Sturmey, P. (2012). Component analysis of behavior skills training in functional analysis. *Behavioral Interventions, 27*, 75–92. doi:10.1002/bin.v27.2

BEHAVIOR CONTRACTS

Bowman-Perrott, L., Burke, M. D., de Marin, S., Zhang, N., & Davis, H. (2015). A meta-analysis of single case research on behavior contracts: Effects on behavioral and academic outcomes among children and youth. *Behavior Modification, 39*(2), 247–269.

Houmanfar, R., Maglieri, K. A., Roman, H. R., & Ward, T. A. (2008). Behavioral contracting. In W. T. O'Donohue & J. E. Fisher (Eds.), *Cognitive behavioural therapy: Applying empirically supported techniques in your practice* (pp. 53–59). Wiley.

Kidd, T. A., & Saudargas, R. A. (1988). Positive and negative consequences in contingency contracts: Their relative effectiveness on arithmetic performance. *Education and Treatment of Children, 11*(2), 118–126.

Miller, D. L., & Kelley, M. L. (1994). The use of goal setting and contingency contracting for improving children's homework performance. *Journal of Applied Behavior Analysis, 27*, 73–84.

Weathers, L., & Liberman, P. (1975). Contingency contracting with families of delinquent adolescents. *Behavior Therapy, 6*, 356–366.

Welch, G. J. (1985). Contingency contracting with a delinquent and his family. *Journal of Behavioral Therapy and Experimental Psychiatry, 16*, 253–259.

USING PRAISE

Dudley, L. L., Axe, J. B., Allen, R. F., & Sweeney-Kerwin, E. J. (2019). Establishing praise as a conditioned reinforcer: Pairing with one versus multiple reinforcers. *Behavioral Interventions, 34*(4), 534–552.

Fefer, S., DeMagistris, J., & Shuttleton, C. (2016). Assessing adolescent praise and reward preferences for academic behavior. *Translational Issues in Psychological Science, 2*(2), 153–162.

Henderlong Corpus, J., & Lepper, M. R. (2007). The effects of person versus performance praise on children's motivation: Gender and age as moderating factors. *Educational Psychology, 27*(4), 487–508.

Hester, P. P., Hendrickson, J. M., & Gable, R. A. (2009). Forty years later: The value of praise, ignoring, and rules for preschoolers at risk for behavior disorders. *Education and Treatment of Children, 32*(4), 513–535.

Owen, D. J., Slep, A. M., & Heyman, R. E. (2012). The effect of praise, positive nonverbal response, reprimand, and negative nonverbal response on child compliance: A systematic review. *Clinical Child and Family Psychology Review, 15*(4), 364–385.

Pomerantz, E. M., & Kempner, S. G. (2013). Mothers' daily person and process praise: Implications for children's theory of intelligence and motivation. *Developmental Psychology, 49*(11), 2040–2046. https://doi.org/10.1037/a0031840

Skinner, B. F. (1969). *Contingencies of reinforcement: A theoretical analysis.* Appleton-Century-Crofts.

Swenson, S., Ho, G. W., Budhathoki, C., Belcher, H. M., Tucker, S., Miller, K., & Gross, D. (2016). Parents' use of praise and criticism in a sample of young children seeking mental health services. *Journal of Pediatric Health Care, 30*(1), 49–56.

POSITIVE BEHAVIOR SUPPORTS AND POSITIVE BEHAVIOR INTERVENTIONS AND SUPPORTS

Bradshaw, C. P., Mitchell, M. M., & Leaf, P. J. (2010). Examining the effects of schoolwide positive behavioral interventions and supports on student outcomes: Results from a randomized controlled effectiveness trial in elementary schools. *Journal of Positive Behavior Interventions, 12*, 133–148.

Bradshaw, C. P., Waasdorp, T. E., & Leaf, P. J. (2012). Effects of school-wide positive behavioral interventions and supports on child behavior problems. *Pediatrics, 130*, 1136–1145.

Dunlap, G., & Horner, R. H. (2006). The applied behavior analytic heritage of PBS: A dynamic model of action-oriented research. *Journal of Positive Behavior Interventions, 8*(1), 58–60.

Horner, R. H., Sugai, G., Smolkowski, K., Eber, L., Nakasato, J., Todd, A. W., & Esperanza, J. (2009). A randomized, wait-list controlled effectiveness trial assessing school-wide positive behavior support in elementary schools. *Journal of Positive Behavior Interventions, 11*, 133–144.

Weiss, M. J., DelPizzo-Cheng, E., LaRue, R. H., & Sloman, K. (2010). ABA and PBS: The dangers in creating artificial dichotomies in behavioral intervention. *The Behavior Analyst Today, 10*(3–4), 428–439.

POSITIVE PSYCHOLOGY

Seligman, M. E. P. (2006). *Learned optimism: How to change your mind and your life.* Random House. (Originally published in 1991 by Alfred A. Knopf.)

Waters, L. (2020). Using positive psychology interventions to strengthen family happiness: A family systems approach. *Journal of Positive Psychology, 15*(5), 645–652. https://doi.org/10.1080/17439760.2020.1789704

Index

Note: Tables and figures are indicated by *t* and *f*, respectively.